Collected Masonic Papers

2013 Transactions
of the
Louisiana Lodge of Research

Collected Masonic Papers

2013 Transactions of the
Louisiana Lodge of Research

MW. Clayton J. Borne, III, 33°, PGM
Worshipful Master
W. Michael R. Poll, PM
Secretary

Published by the Louisiana Lodge of Research
by agreement with
Cornerstone Book Publishers
Copyright as a collection © 2013 by Louisiana Lodge of Research
http://louisianalodgeofresearch.org

Cornerstone Book Publishers
New Orleans, LA
www.cornerstonepublishers.com

ISBN: 1613421435
ISBN-13: 978-1-61342-143-7

MADE IN THE USA

Table of Contents

Past Masters of the Louisiana Lodge of Research

1989-90: William J. Mollere
1991: Ballard L. Smith
1992: Irving I. Berglass
1993: Philip J. Walker, Jr
1994: Beryl C. Franklin
1995: Ernest C. Belmont, Jr
1996: Thomas P. Brown
1997: Larry H. Moore
1998: Darrell L. Aldridge
1999: Edward W. Brabham, Jr
2000: Howard F. Entwistle, Jr
2001: Johnnie K. Hill
2002: Richard L. James
2003: Terrell Howes
2004: Glenn Cupit
2005: Robert Bazzell
2006: John Bellanger
2007: Jimmy Leger
2008: Ion Lazar
2009: Bill Richards
2010: Ricks Bowles
2011-13: Clayton J. Borne, III

The Grand Lodge of Louisiana, F&AM
P.O. Box 12357
5746 Masonic Drive
Alexandria, Louisiana. 71315-2357
Website: http://www.la-mason.com

M:W: H. Edward Durham
Grand Master
R:W: Earl J. "Mickey" Durand
Deputy Grand Master
R:W: William J. Mollere
Grand Senior Warden
R:W: Will P. Gray
Grand Junior Warden
M:W: Woody Bilyeu, PGM
Grand Treasurer
M:W: Roy B. Tuck, Jr., P.G.M.
Grand Secretary

Collected Masonic Papers

x

Language of the Heart

by Carl H. Claudy

FREEMASONRY TEACHES BY SYMBOLS!

WHY? Why does she veil in allegory and conceal in an object or picture a meaning quite different from its name?

Why should Freemasonry express Immortality with Acacia, Brotherly Love with a Trowel, the World by a Lodge and Right Living by a Mason's

That Freemasonry conceals in symbols in order to arouse curiosity to know their meaning is often considered the only explanation. But there are many more lofty ideas of why this great system of truth, philosophy and ethics is hidden in symbols.

It is hardly a matter of argument that man has a triple nature; he has a body and senses which bring him into contact with and translate the meanings of the physical world of earth, air, fire and water which is about him. He has a brain and a mind by which he reasons and understands about the matters physical with which he is surrounded. And he has a Something Beyond; call it Soul, Heart, Spirit or imagination, as you will; it is something which is allied to, rather than a part of reason, and connected with the physical side of life only through its sensory contacts.

This soul, or spirit, comprehends a language which the brain does not understand. The keenest minds have striven without success to make this mystic language plain to reason. When you hear music which brings tears to your eyes and grief or joy to your heart, you respond to a language your brain does not understand and cannot explain. It is not with your brain that you love your mother, your child or your wife; it is with the Something Beyond; and the language with which that love is spoken is not the language of the tongue.

A symbol is a word in that language. Translate that symbol into words which appeal only to the mind, and the spirit of the meaning is lost. Words appeal to the mind; meanings not expressed in words appeal to the spirit.

All that there is in Freemasonry, which can be set down in words on a page, leaves out completely the Spirit of the Order, If we depend upon words or ideas alone, the Fraternity would not make a universal appeal to all men, since no man has it given to him to appeal to minds of all other men. But Freemasonry expresses truths which are universal; it expresses them in a universal language, universally understood by all men without words. That language is the language of the symbol, and the symbol is universally understood because it is the means of communication between spirit, souls and hearts.

When we say of Masonry that it is universal we mean the word literally; it is of the universe, not merely of the world. If it were possible for an inhabitant of Mars to make and use a telescope which would enable him to plainly see a square mile of the surface of the earth, and if we knew it and desired to, we could draw upon that square mile a symbol to communicate with that inhabitant of Mars, we would choose, undoubtedly, one with as many meanings as possible; one which had a material, mental and spiritual meaning. Such a symbol might be the triangle, the square or the circle. Our supposed Martian might respond with a complimentary symbol; if we showed him a triangle he might reply with the 47th Problem. If we showed him a circle he might send down 3.141659 - the number by which a diameter is multiplied to become the circumference. We could find a language in symbols with which to begin a communication, even with all the universe!

Naturally then, Freemasonry employs symbols for heart to speak to heart. Imagination is the heart's collection of senses. So we must appeal to the imagination when speaking a truth which is neither mental nor physical, and the symbol is the means by which one imaginations speaks to another. Nothing else will do; no words can be as effective (unless they are themselves symbols); no teachings expressed in language can be as easily learned by the heart as those which come via the symbol through the imagination.

Take from Masonry its symbols and you have just the husk; the kernel is gone. He who hears but the words of Freemasonry misses their meaning entirely. Most symbols have many interpretations. These do not contradict but amplify each other. Thus, the square is a symbol of perfection, rectitude of conduct, honor, honesty and good work. There are all different and yet allied. The square is not a symbol of wrong, evil, meanness or disease! Ten different men may read ten different meanings into a square, and yet each meaning fits with and belongs to the other meanings.

Ten men have ten different kinds of hearts. Not all have the same power of imagination. They do not all have the same ability to comprehend. So each gets from a symbol what he can. He uses his imagination. He translates to his soul as much of the truth as he is able to make a part of him. This the ten cannot do with truths expressed in words. "Twice two is equal to four" is a truth which must be accepted all at once, as a complete exposition, or not at all. He who can not understand the "twice" or the "equal" or the "four" has no conception of what is being said. But ten men can read ten progressive, different, correct and beautiful meanings into a trowel, and each can be right as far as he goes. The man who sees it merely as an instrument which helps to bind has a part of its meaning. He who finds it a link with operative Masons has another part. The man who sees it as a symbol of man's relationship to Deity, because with it he (spiritually) does the Master's Work, has another meaning. All these meanings are right; when all men know all the meanings the need for Freemasonry will have passed away.

We use symbols because only by them can we speak the language of the spirit, each to each, and because they form an elastic language, which each man reads for himself according to his ability. Symbols form the only language which is thus elastic, and the only one by which spirit can be touched. To suggest that Freemasonry use any other would be as revolutionary as to remove her Altars, meet in a Public Square or elect by majority vote. Freemasonry without symbols would not be Freemasonry; it would be but a dogmatic and not very erudite philosophy, of which the world is full of as it is, and none of which ever satisfies the heart.

The Scottish Rite Bicentennial Academic Symposium: Reflections in Louisiana History

by Clayton J. Borne, III, 33°, PGM
Worshipful Master, Louisiana Lodge of Research
Presented at the Scottish Rite Bicentennial Academic Symposium - June 1, 2, 3, and 4, 2011. New Orleans, LA

GRAND MASTERS, Sovereign Grand Commanders, Sovereign Grand Inspectors General, Commanders in Chief, Ladies and Gentlemen, and Brothers all, Good Evening, I trust that you would share in my sentiments that considering the historical evidence presented at this Bicentennial (1811-2011) Academic Symposium, we can be extremely proud of the dominant role that Louisiana has played in the development of our beloved Scottish Rite of Free Masonry.

The factual evidence is clear that by the early 1800s, the Masonic discipline had firmly established itself in Louisiana. Two distinct mainstreams or traditions were clearly identifiable with three dominant Rites: The American or York Rite Masonry; The French or Modern Rite Masonry; and The Scottish Rite of Free Masonry. Our early lodges — Perfect Union Lodge #1, Etoile Polaire Lodge #1, and Perseverance Lodge #4 — have unique histories that are interesting examples of these influences.

Perfect Union was established under a French Rite authority, chartered under a York Rite authority and had a Scottish Rite Lodge merged into its numbers: Bienfassance Lodge #1 originally chartered out of the Grand Consistory of the Supreme Council at Kingston, Jamaica in 1807.

Etoile Polaire Lodge, at one time, actually held three authorities — York Rite, French Rite, and The Scottish Rite. Communications were held with meetings convening on different nights each under a different authority or charter. Initially in our history to adhere to a different persuasion or discipline was no impediment to the recognition of Masons and the practice of our art.

Dr. Jean-Jacques Jambroski of the Grand Lodge of France recounted how these movements migrated to the French colonies in the Americas, specifically Martinique, San Domingo, and Jamaica and how the higher degrees were created as elaborations upon the three symbolic degrees of British Craft Masonry.

W. Bro. Marc Conrad tendered conclusive evidence that the ritual of our Modern Scottish Rite was developed in the Louisiana Supreme Council. These expansive additions or higher degrees to the ritual were viewed by some as a superior form of Masonry. These Scottish Rite proponents advocated advancement into these higher degrees and believed that the advanced enlightenment accentuated the separation or divisions created in any given society.

This was not a new concept. The ancient philosopher Plato in his dialogue "The Republic" articulates and embraces a belief in a natural inequality of man in that all men are not created equal. Some men are better than others in that their wills are more capable of striving for excellence and the integrity to do what must be done as opposed to those that express weakness of will. It is the theme of our "Spiritual Brotherhood" and the motivation for our continuing "Search for Light." The object of this discipline is to encourage the betterment of one's self and in due course the betterment of all of mankind.

This philosophy I truly believe must be made clear in order to understand the development of 18th century French or Scottish Rite Masonry.

The Sharp-Bordeaux documents discovered in Bordeaux, France, in 1928, now made available to us through the dedicated efforts of W. Bro. Michael Poll and his Cornerstone Book Publishers, clearly established that the earliest of these degrees were brought to the French Islands of the Caribbean sometime prior to 1750, and subsequently to New Orleans by charter in 1752. This was long before the much publicized Brother Etienne (Stephen) Morin's 1761 patent to establish the Rite of Perfection in the Caribbean on the Island of Hispaniola (Dominican Republic and Haiti).

Louisiana's rich Masonic history began with the birth of its mother lodge in 1738. It was named Perfect Union Lodge and was located on the Island of Martinique in the Lesser Antilles. That lodge was constituted by the Grand Lodge of France and reconstituted by the Grand Orient in 1775. In the *"Sharp-Bordeaux Documents,"* it was recorded that this Lodge proudly called herself the "Granddaughter of Clermont" and daughter of Very Worshipful and Perfect Ecossois Lodge at Bordeaux, France.

The most significant date however was on July 16, 1752. This Perfect Union Lodge in Martinique chartered a Lodge in New Orleans named Perfect Harmonie. The earliest document being a letter dated 1750 confirms Masonic activity operations in the City during the 1740s. This Lodge was the first evidence of organized Masonry in the Louisiana Territory and, more specifically, in New Orleans. The documented evidence is found in the following:

Sharp-Bordeaux Document #40-I

> *"From the Orient, in a place, where reigns the concord, the silence, the Peace and La Parfaite Union, the year of the Great Light 5752, and the 3rd Sunday, 16th of the month July.*
> *"Rules and Special Laws (Constitution and By-Laws,) which the Wor. Lodge La Parfaite Union de la Martinique, granddaughter of Clermont, sends to the Wor. Lodge de la Parfaite Harmonie of New Orleans, province of Louisiana, to which she has to conform with the pleasure of the Constitutions, which have empowered her, upon the request, which has been made to her by the deputation to this Wor. Lodge, in the person of the Bro. Fooks, Perfect Ecossais, Pierre Caresse, master Mason, and Bro. Louis Batard, Master Mason, all members of the above-mentioned Wor. Lodge La Parfaite Harmonie."*

The established etiquette of putting a brothers highest Masonic rank or degree following his name clearly establishing or proves brothers with degrees of the higher grade, existing in New Orleans in 1752. The Sharp-Bordeaux document #40-1, confirms Bro. Fooks as a Perfect Ecossais Mason.

This uncontradicted evidence clearly established and documented New Orleans as the first Jurisdiction of Masonry" on the North American continent wherein the primitive higher degrees are found.

On April 12, 1764, the reconstituted charter of Perfect Harmony in New Orleans was to have arrived in which the Lodge was reconstituted as an "Elus Parfait d'Ecosse" (Perfect Elect Ecossais) Lodge. This was four years before Francken established the ineffable lodge at Albany, New York, in 1768. It was further written that a Lodge "La Consolante Masconne" was established in New Orleans on July 16, 1765, which received a charter from Lodge Anglaise de Bordeaux, France. Shortly thereafter, these lodges merely disappeared from recorded history.

This writer believes, as confirmed by historical events of the day explain the disappearance of these lodges. France was experiencing severe problems in its attempts to keep its island possession of Santa Domingo and La Martinique and to recapture Guadeloupe. Neither Antoine Crozat, John Law, nor the company of the Indies in their proprietary relationship with France were able to make the Louisiana holdings profitable. In order to gain the financial stability needed to achieve their objectives, on November 3, 1762, France ceded by the secret Treaty of Fountainebleu, New Orleans and the "Isle of Orleans," the Florida parishes, and the whole of Louisiana west of the Mississippi River to Spain. Spain knew of the colonies' economic hardship; however, they saw the acquisition as a territorial buffer to their western holdings.

In 1766, upon the arrival of the first Spanish Governor, Don Antonio Ulloa, the French population began a desperate revolt. As confirmed by the Sharp-Bordeaux Documents, many city leaders were leaders in the Masonic Fraternity, such as Bros. Jean Milhet, Foucault, Villere and Doucet, Tiphaine, Caresse, and Rousselon. Escorting Gov. Ulloa out of the city. These city leaders proclaimed independence. By definition, New Orleans was for a short time an Independent Republic.

In 1769, a Spanish officer of Irish decent, Governor O'Reilly, arrived in New Orleans with an army to reestablish Spanish Civil authority. On October 24, 1769, our Masonic brothers La Freniere, Hogan, Villere, Marquis, and Milhet were arrested and, after a trial, were executed, Other leaders, without trials, were imprisoned. They included Tiphaine, Guillaume, Rousselon, and Caresse. It was truly a Holy Inquisition that persecuted Freemasonry and put an end to recorded Masonic communications until emergence of Perfect Union Lodge in 1793 and Etoile Potraie in 1794 in New Orleans.

Etoile Polaire Lodge #1, which will be hosting an open house for the Symposium attendees tomorrow, has records dating to 1796. The language and records of the early premier lodge remained in French until 1957, when the lodge held its last meeting in the French language with only a few brothers maintaining their native language. Fast forwarding through the reacquisition of Louisiana by France from Spain and the 1803 French Louisiana Purchase by the United States.

We celebrate today the arrival and establishment of the 1811 Grand Consistory of Louisiana chartered out of the Supreme Council at Kingston, Jamaica, which was established by Degrasse Tilley in 1802. To date, there are no known records of this premier body, only supporting documentation namely: 1) a communication dated April 20, 1811 from the Sov. Grand Consistory of Princes of the Royal Secret to Etoile Polaire Lodge; 2) also in Albert Pike's 1882 "Official Bulletin" he give a narrative of the formation of this body, along with a roster. Examples being P.F. DuBorg (First Grand Master of the 1812 Grand Lodge of Louisiana), Jean Soulie (Second Grand Master of the 1812 Grand Lodge of Louisiana), T. Urquart (Mayor of the City of New Orleans), Christian Miltenberger (New Orleans Banker), and others. The Louisiana Supreme Council, is also to have has letters of notification of this establishment of the 1811 Grand Consistory in their archives.

In 1812 the Grand Lodge for the State of Louisiana was formed. Many of the same names appearing in Pike's writing of the 1811 Grand Consistory were the dominate names in the formation of the Grand Lodge. In addition, Louisiana became a state in 1812. Interestingly, in 1813, another Grand Consistory is formed and the Louisiana body looked to New York not Charleston for its authority. More likely than not this was the result of the "Ancient" "Modern" struggles in Charleston with the ever-present issue of "regularity."

In 1839, a Supreme Council of the AASR was created in New Orleans. From 1836 New Orleans was a staging city for men and financing for the Texas War for independency, a topic on which one of our Symposium lecturers, W. Bro. Pete Normand, is the authority. With the influx of Americans into New Orleans, the French culture ran head long into conflict and the two societies clashed.

By 1847, however, the whole of Louisiana Freemasonry was divided along cultural and jurisdictional lines. Louisiana Freemasonry had been created by French Masons and our Freemasonry, as well as the society in general, was French in nature - this included the Supreme Council. The initial impact resulted in the creation of two grand lodges. The Americans influence became dominant and the French culture as well as French Masonry fell from favor.

In 1850, the French styled Grand Lodge of Louisiana merged with a Grand Lodge created in New Orleans in 1847 only a few years prior by those advocating the York Rite or "American" interests. The "new"

1850 Grand Lodge of Louisiana became more inline with the rest of the US Grand Lodges. Lost was the French domination and control of Louisiana Masonry.

In 1855, about half of the Active Members of the Supreme Council created in New Orleans signed a "Concordat" with the Supreme Council in Charleston, SC. The New Orleans Valley, your host for this symposium, is the continuation of the body created by that Concordat. The Active Members of the Louisiana Supreme Council in New Orleans who did not participate in the Concordat of 1855 remained and some of that body are with us tonight. We believe this effort of cooperation by these two bodies for the Bicentennial Celebration to be an historic moment in the history of the Scottish Rite. Our sincerest appreciation to Grand Commander Washington, and Grand Commander Seal for their dynamic leadership.

Disapproving of the "Concordat," Judge James Foulhouze (Grand Commander from 1848-1853) reportedly gathered together a number of the remaining 33rds in New Orleans. Grand Commander Foulhouze continued to serve as Acting Grand Commander of the Supreme Council of Louisiana until the election of J.J.E. Massicott as Sovereign Grand Commander in October, 1856. The Supreme Council of Louisiana has proudly continued to exist.

There is no evidence that Fraternal relations between this divided body currently the Supreme Council of Louisiana and the Supreme Council, SJ ever met again. Our Academic Symposium is a dynamic milestone for our beloved Scottish Rite in New Orleans with the meeting of the two bodies for a common effort of education, respect, and fellowship.

Our history further shows that from 1839 until 1850, many of the offices of the Grand Lodge of Louisiana with most all Grand Masters were 33rds under the Supreme Council of Louisiana. One Past Grand Master, Jean-François Canonge, a member of my mother lodge Perfect Union Lodge #1, served as Grand Commander (1845-1848) just prior to The Honorable Judge James Foulhouze.

As confirmed by W. Bro. Marc Conrad's research of Sov. Grand Commander Albert Pike's writings that the present degree structure of the SJ along with a number of the Pike rituals were the result of and had their origins in the New Orleans Scottish Rite arena with Grand Commander Foulhouze as the author. Even the method of election of officers and advancing the number of Active Members in the Supreme Council above the original nine came from the already existing practice of the Supreme Council in New Orleans. Regardless of all other questions, much of what we know today as the AASR was originated in New Orleans by its Supreme Council. We are proud of our rich dynamic Scottish Rite history.

In conclusion, the principles of our Masonic Brotherhood with its principled philosophy has been embraced over the course of history and has been identified with diverse social movements of which New Orleans is a classic example. From ultra-conservatives to utopian socialist all found a moral principle embraced in the teachings of the brotherhood that gave their cause credibility and Universal Appeal.

Our Scottish Rite of Freemasonry relentlessly moved for the recognition of the rights of man, the endless battle against blind ignorance, uncompromising intolerance, emotional superstition and human error. But where is the basic common bond in the Universal Brotherhood? What are the basic elements and the fundamental principles that bonded men of all ages together attempting to insure the basis for a disciplined social order?

I believe that our fraternity is the result of no one identifiable institution or school of thought, but rather a philosophical and spiritual movement emerging in Ancient Artesian Societies where man is seen individually and collectively confronting his humanness in an attempt to understand himself and his place in the universe. It is the challenge of viewing human existence played out in life by the struggle between the powers of evil relentlessly confronting through temptation the divine principles of good.

This philosophy fostered, even in the most ancient times, the principles of character: Truth, Morality, and Brotherly Love. As is often stated, the Masonic philosophy, more particularly the Scottish Rite discipline fosters a Brotherhood of Man under the Fatherhood of God.

I leave you with the thought expressed at a meeting of a Scottish Rite body which subsequently appearing in a New Orleans newspaper in the late 1870 following the Civil War, upon the installation of Ernest St. Cyr WM of Fraternal Lodge #20 chartered out of the "Supreme Council of the General Inspectors of the 33° of The Scottish Rite of the Sovereign and Independent State of Louisiana":

"In spite of all the old prejudice, the Scottish Rite Masons have taken the initiative to unfurl the banner of 'fraternity and equality' under that glorious fold so much good may be accomplished."

The Scottish Rite Bicentennial Academic Symposium held here in New Orleans this June 1, 2, 3, and 4, 2011 brings together brethrens representing The Supreme Council of Louisiana, the Supreme Council SJUSA, The Supreme Council of France, The Supreme Council NMJ USA, Grand Lodge of Louisiana and the Grand Lodge of France is a dynamic accomplishment of our beloved Scottish Rite.

A Masonic Metamorphosis

by Dr. Lawrence D. Wade, MD,PM
St. James Lodge #47

ONE of Louisiana's newest Masonic Lodges, "The Lodge of the Nine Muses, No. 9, F. & A. M." (LoNM) – very likely the most formal of all Louisiana Lodges – began as an informal Masonic "Discussion Group" – The Baton Rouge Masonic Forum (a.k.a. "The Baton Rouge Area Masonic Forum", "The Masonic Scholars' Discussion Group", or "The Discussion Group".)

The Caterpillar – "The Discussion Group" –

It was on Saturday, February 5, 2000, in Shreveport, that I first attended a meeting of the Louisiana Lodge of Research. I had been a Mason for four years. At that meeting, Bro. Naresh Sharma presented an excellent paper on, "Evolution of the Ritual".

After the meeting, I was loitering outside the motel entrance, when Bro. Sharma – not yet a non-smoker, at that time – stepped out to smoke a cigarette. In the course of our conversation, Bro. Sharma suggested that Baton Rouge Masons needed a meeting of some sort in which to discuss shared interests such as the history of The Craft, philosophical aspects of the Fraternity, etc. Bro. Sharma encouraged me to get out some e-mail messages to area Masons and to check with restaurants on the availability and the affordability of meeting rooms.

Responses from Baton Rouge area Masons were generally very favorable. Fifteen Masons attended our first meeting – on March 22, 2000, at Giamanco's Restaurant - at which WB Sharma presented an excellent paper on, "The William Morgan Affair".

That first meeting was on the fourth Wednesday of the month; subsequent meetings were always on the second Wednesday. At the second meeting, Bro. Bill Moliere presented a well-researched paper on, "The Development of Masonry in Southeast Louisiana"; again, fifteen Masons were in attendance.

From the beginning, we agreed not to meet in December. The average number attending the eight meetings held during calendar year 2000 was 16.4, with a high of 22 and a low of 11. Over the first twelve months, a total of 42 Masons attended at least one of our meetings. In addition to Bro. Sharma and Bro. Moliere, presenters during the year 2000 included Bro. Larry Moore, Bro. Carle Jackson, Bro. Larry Wade, Bro. Guy Beck, and Bro. Ernie Easterly. Other presenters in subsequent years have included WB Lenton Sartain, WB Donald Park, a sitting Grand Master (MW Patrick Kelly) and three other members of the Grand Court (RWB John Beaumont, RWB Bro. Chip Borne, and RWB Joe Cabuk – though in the case of RWB Cabuk, the birth of a grandchild in a distant state made it necessary for Bro. Sharma to read his excellent paper in the absence of its author.)

Of the approximately thirty papers written for presentation to "The Discussion Group," a number have been published in official statewide Masonic journals such as "The Louisiana Freemason" and "The Scottish Rite Trestleboard".

Papers presented to the group have ranged over a broad scope of Masonic topics.

In addition to topics related to the history of Freemasonry, there have been papers on Masonic Renewal, Membership Development, Masonic Leadership/Growth, and the future of The Craft. During his year as GM, MW Patrick Kelly honored The Discussion Group by appearing in person and discussing his views on the future of Freemasonry; at a subsequent meeting, Bro. Ronnie Seale shared his views on this subject, as well.

There have been several papers on, for example, the development of Freemasonry in Southeast Louisiana, the history of French Masonry in Louisiana, and Masonry's role in The American Revolution.

Two papers discussed Masonic Symbolism – one, its theoretical aspects and one, its practical significance. One other paper analyzed the Entered Apprentice Degree from a fresh perspective; another studied "The Ancient Landmarks"; another "The Prestonian Lectures"; and yet another "The Anderson Constitutions".

Two books reviewed in separate presentations to the Discussion Group were *Revolutionary Brotherhood* and *Bowling Alone.*

The negatives of William Morgan and Leo Taxil were more than balanced by the positives of Bro. John Philip Sousa and Bro. W. A. Mozart, plus a comprehensive review of U. S. Presidents who were Freemasons.

At a unique juncture in American history – the invasion of Afghanistan by American military forces, in response to the World Trade Center tragedy of 9/11/01 – The Discussion Group meeting of 08/14/02 featured a presentation on, "Afghanistan – History and Current Status", by Mr. Henry Bradsher, a former Associated Press Moscow Bureau Chief and CIA operative and a noted expert on Afghanistan, who has authored many published articles on the subject, including several current encyclopedia entries. This meeting was very well attended and was taken as one of our most successful events.

Two meetings were devoted to the study of Mysticism and Masonry, Kabalistic and beyond; two to The Temple Mount; and several (as stated) to Masonic Renewal, Membership Issues, and The Future of Freemasonry.

The Metamorphosis – Table Lodge –

By March of 2003, Bro. and Mrs. Ricks Bowles had moved to Baton Rouge from Minnesota, and Bro. Ricks had joined the Discussion Group. In Minnesota, Bro. Bowles had been a member of St. Paul Lodge #3 - a formal European-style Table Lodge. One of our members, Bro. Paul Roberts, had sat in Lodge at that Lodge. On Wednesday, March 12, 2003, the Masonic Forum sponsored its first "Table Lodge", with W. Bro. Gaylord Strand, PM of St Paul Lodge #3, as guest speaker.

The second "Table Lodge" took place on November 12, 2003. This time, the meeting was open to wives and guests, and the featured speaker was the internationally renowned UCLA Professor of History, Dr. Margaret Jacob, author of *Living the Enlightenment: Freemasonry and Politics in Eighteenth-Century Europe*, a number of other very authoritative books on the history of Freemasonry, and more than forty articles in major historical journals. Dr. Jacob serves on the editorial boards of numerous important journals of professional historians. This meeting was attended by more than 100 members and guests and was an unqualified success.

Of course, these "Table Lodges" were not tyled Lodges. The success of these meetings, however, along with the fact that "Discussion Group" members were generally quite receptive to the concept, lent impetus to the notion of transitioning from informal

"Discussion Group" to formal European-style "Table Lodge". Under a succession of Grand Masters, the Grand Lodge was supportive.

The Butterfly Takes Flight – "Lodge of the Nine Muses" –

Not only is LoNM one of Louisiana's newest Lodges – it is at once one of the most innovative and one of the most traditional Lodges. It is innovative, in fact, in the very manner in which it reverts, in every respect, to tradition – to the traditional formality, that is, of European Freemasonry.

This Lodge was originally the brainchild of Bro. Naresh Sharma, Bro. William Mollere, and Bro. Ernest Easterly, with subsequent assistance and leadership from Bro. Ricks Bowles The name, "Lodge of the Nine Muses", is taken, of course, from the Lodge in Paris at which WB Benjamin Franklin, in 1778, conducted the Enlightenment philosopher, Voltaire, through the Degrees of Freemasonry, just a few months before the death of Bro. Voltaire.

Formality is evident from the moment one arrives for the meeting. Everyone in attendance is in formal attire – mostly in tuxedos, with a few, perhaps, in dark business suits, instead. Attendance is limited to members and invited guests. Membership is restricted to those Masons who will support and comply with the requirement that they must be willing to research, prepare, and present scholarly papers on subjects germane to Freemasonry, the requirement that they attend all meetings, and other similar requirements

While its monthly meetings are tyled meetings, LoNM has continued the tradition of annual "Table Lodge" meetings, open to family members and invited guests. The 2005 Table Lodge was held on Wednesday, November 9th. The speaker was WB Robert Davis, Secretary of the Guthrie, Oklahoma Scottish Rite Valley. Bro. Davis is a well-known and respected Masonic scholar, author and speaker. The 2006 Table Lodge was held on Friday, November 3rd. The speaker, from Washington, DC, was Baton Rouge's own WB Ronald A Seale, Sovereign Grand Commander of the Supreme Council of the Southern Jurisdiction of the Scottish Rite of Freemasonry.

Throughout its first year, LoNM was "UD" – "Under Dispensation". In its wisdom, the GL soon granted a charter and, further, agreed to allow the Lodge to bring out of retirement the designation, "No. 9". Thus was born The Lodge of the Nine Muses, No. 9, F&AM.

A bittersweet sidebar is related to the delivery of the Lodge's charter. At the time, one of our beloved members, RWB James Pecoraro, was dying of cancer. Though Bro. Jim had been an active participant in the "Discussion Group", his actual petition for membership in LoNM was, for understandable reasons, delayed. And, though it was entirely inadvertent, his name was not included in the list of charter members, when the charter was first printed. Was it by the hand of The Supreme Grand Architect of the Universe, that the printer was guided to also misspell the word "Masonry" as "Masonary", thus assuring that it would be necessary that the charter be reprinted? Whatever the case, we were all deeply joyful that his dear friend (and fellow LoNM Charter Member), Bro. Glenn Cupit, was able to confidently assure Bro. Jim on his deathbed that his name would quite definitely be included, after all, among those listed on the charter, itself, as charter members of LoNM.

In a Craft that many Masons see as INCLUSIVE, welcoming all men who believe in the Brotherhood of Men under the Fatherhood of God, the EXCLUSIVE appearance that arises from the formality and from the restrictions on membership and attendance is viewed as objectionable, at best, and unMasonic at worst.

To members and supporters of LoNM, however, the constraints and restrictions applied to membership and to attendance represent, instead, the principles of Freemasonry refined and advanced beyond their ordinary day-to-day interpretation and application LoNM focuses heavily on the notion of "Making Good Men Better" – of having its members find and express the best in themselves and in their brethren.

Ancient Greek philosophers held that while perfection is not achievable, it should be a man's purpose to be a slightly better man today than yesterday and slightly better tomorrow than today. It is, perhaps, this principle, more than any other, that guides and sustains LoNM.

The Templar Degrees of
The Ancient & Accepted Scottish Rite of Freemasonry

by *Pierre G. Normand, Jr., 33°*
Founding Member, Fellow, and Former Editor, Scottish Rite Research Society
Former Chairman, Scottish Rite Valley of Houston

THE Order of the Temple of Solomon. "The Poor Fellow-soldiers of Christ and the Temple of Solomon," better known as "The Knights Templar," or "The Order of the Temple of Solomon," were a religious military order during the 12th, 13th and early 14th centuries. Prior to their formation, so-called "orders of knighthood" were unknown. Religious orders consisted of monks and canons, but did not include soldiers or knights. But, in 1129, with the sponsorship of Bernard of Clairvaux, Abbot of the Cistercian Order, the Council of Troyes granted recognition to the Templars as a religious military order – warrior monks.

Over the next two centuries the Order became the largest and wealthiest army in the world. Their wealth and power incurred the jealousy of King Phillip IV of France who ordered the arrest of the Templars in Paris on Friday, 13 October 1307. A Papal Bull ordered the arrest of all Templars, who were then tortured and forced to confess to false charges. After the trials, the Pope dissolved the Order in 1312. The last Grand Master of the Order, Jacques DeMolay, and the Preceptor of Normandy, Geoffrey de Charney, were burned at the stake in front of Notre Dame Cathedral on 18 March 1314.

The Supreme Council, Thirty-Third Degree, of the Ancient & Accepted Scottish Rite of Freemasonry, a neo-Templar organization, represents the spiritual, if not the historic, survival of the Knights Templar, and that is evident in its hierarchical structure, in the titles of its officers, and in its regalia. Demonstrative of its Templar character, the six highest and last degrees conferred by the Scottish Rite are all Knight Templar degrees, more than by any other regular rite of Freemasonry.

28th Degree: Knight Commander of the Temple. The Traditional History of the Degree, which forms a part of the ritual of the degree, preserves the legend of the survival of "The Knights of the Temple of Solomon" in Germany. This history begins with the siege at Acre in 1191, and continues through the official dissolution of the Templars in 1312, and the subsequent absorption of Templar survivors by the Teutonic Order, where the Templars were permitted to adopt the red mantle with black cross as it now appears in this Degree.

29th Degree: Scottish Knight of St. Andrew. (The Traditional History of the Order gives the history of the Knights Templar from their formation in the year 1118, through their betrayal in 1307, and the trial and martyrdom of their Grand Master in 1314. It further preserves the legend of their alliance with King Robert the Bruce of Scotland at the Battle of Bannockburn, St. John's Day, 1314, where was defeated the English army of King Edward II.

To commemorate their service, King Robert Bruce created, and received these knights into, the Scottish Order of St. Andrew du Chardon, meaning "of the Thistle". The History of the Order states that the hereditary Grand Mastership of the Order passed down from King Robert the Bruce in succession through the Stuart Royal family to Prince Charles Edward Stuart, the last Grand Master in Scotland, who, after his defeat by the English in 1745, escaped into exile in France and established there a Chapter of Rosé Croix of Heredom which encompassed the Order of St. Andrew.

The Order was in the possession of the founders of the Ancient & Accepted Scottish Rite of Freemasonry at its formation in 1801, at which time the legend of the Degree was still combined with the Rosé Croix as a part of the 18th Degree. It was subsequently separated from the 18th Degree and moved to its present position as the 29th Degree.

30th Degree: Knight Kadosh of the White and Black Eagle. The drama of this degree takes place after the death of the twenty-first and last Grand Master of the Knights Templar, Jacques DeMolay.

His initials, "J.B.M." are evident upon his tomb, upon the shield of a Knight Kadosh, and upon the Cross of the Order. During the degree, the Beauseant, the white and black standard of the Order, is prominently displayed. Among the officers of a Council, or

Preceptory, of the Order are bearers of the White Standard, the Black Standard, and the Beauseant.

The Commander of Knights Kadosh opens a Council with the words, "Knights of the Holy House of the Temple, poor fellow soldiers of the Temple of Solomon...." In the reception of a candidate for the Degree he is referred to as "one who aspires to the rank of Knight Kadosh, or Knight of the Temple." The Hebrew word "Kadosh" means "holy", "pure", or "separated."

The history of the medieval Knights Templar is a treasured part of the Degree, although often abbreviated during conferrals. It preserves the legend of the survival of the Templars and their traditions in the Masonic degrees of the Scottish Rite, of the duplicity of the rival Knights of St. John, the Hospitalers, also called the Knights of Malta, who profited from the fall of the Templars, of the Hospitalers persecution of Freemasonry as late as the mid-1700s, and of the special enmity reserved for the Order of Malta by the Knights Kadosh.

In the mid-eighteenth century, the Kadosh Degree was the 24th of the 25-degree Order of the Royal Secret, the immediate predecessor of the Scottish Rite. At the formation of the Scottish Rite in 1801, the Kadosh Degree was listed as the 29th, and was later moved to the 30th.

31st Degree: Grand Inspector Inquisitor Commander. This is the second of the three "Kadosh Degrees" of the Scottish Rite. In The Scottish Rite Manifesto of 1802, this degree, along with the 30th and 32nd are listed simply as "Prince of the Royal Secret." The Degree represents the judiciary of the Order of Knights Templar, and it has always been utilized as the final test of the candidate before he is admitted to the Thirty-Second Degree.

After the suppression of the Knights Templar it was imperative that one claiming to be a fugitive knight seeking refuge in a Templar asylum where he was not known be tested fully to determine if he was worthy, and not a spy or enemy of the Order. In one early version of the Degree, the candidate was tested in his knowledge of the eight degrees of Entered Apprentice, Fellow-Craft, Master Mason, [Perfect] Elect Mason, Scottish Master, Knight of the East, Sovereign Prince Rosé Croix, and Knight Kadosh, before being permitted to advance. The "Court of the Dead" from Egyptian mythology is an allegory for this final judgment, and is the final test of the initiate before he is given The Royal Secret.

32nd Degree: Master of the Royal Secret. (The third of the Kadosh degrees of the Scottish Rite, its object is to gather together all the degrees of the Scottish Rite into the Symbolic Camp. The costume of a Master of the Royal Secret is that of a Knight.

Kadosh, and the Knights Kadosh are the legitimate successors of the medieval Knights Templar. The distinctive Scottish Rite cap is the last vestige of the chivalric regalia of a Kadosh of the Thirty-Second Degree. In the Legenda of the Thirty-Second Degree we are taught that "only by constant labor in the daily walks of life … can the Knights Kadosh become the true soldiery of the Holy House of the Temple of Solomon." In "The Readings of the 32nd Degree" we find "The Templar Dogma," wherein is explained the war *à outrance* between Light and Darkness.

33rd Degree: Inspector General. Conferred only by the Supreme Council, 33°, the Degree of Inspector General is a Templar degree throughout, in both substance and symbolism. The officers of the Supreme Council are the officers of a Grand Preceptory of Knights Templar, presided over by a Grand Commander. The symbol of the Grand Commander, the Salem Cross with crosslets, is the symbol of the Grand Master of Knights Templar.

The fact that the Scottish Rite is the spiritual descendant of "The Poor Fellow Soldiery of the Temple of Solomon" (The Order of Knights Templar), is best betrayed, however, in the full name of the Mother Supreme Council, which is "The Supreme Council of the Inspectors General Knights Commanders of <u>The House of the Temple of Solomon</u> of the Thirty-Third and Last Degree of the Ancient and Accepted Scottish Rite of Freemasonry."

DeMolay

by Clayton J. Borne, III, 33°, PGM
Worshipful Master, Louisiana Lodge of Research

WHAT in particular impressed you about your Masonic obligation? Do you believe that it demands a life of self reflection? A standard of conduct that will influence others by living a virtuous life, a life that will set you apart, a life with a disciplined purpose? If so, could that obligation or discipline extend to being a leader of our youth? I truly believe that it does. It is a natural progression of your continuing search for light. It requires a unique commitment to patience, wisdom, the ability to think and act young, to communicate with the younger generation in a manner to establish confidence and a life with disciplined principles. It is a life with purpose, a life with moral integrity. A youth fraternity dedicated to such principles was the vision of a dedicated 33rd degree Scottish Rite Mason of many years past, Frank S. Land, founder of DeMolay.

Frank S. Land, in establishing a Fraternal Organization for young men was preaching his own convictions-the principles of a good life, the philosophy his family had instilled in him. His hope was to establish a fraternity of young men, committed to the ideals of being better sons, better citizens, and better leaders. His desire would be to develop leaders that would hold true to their ideals not just in the good times when all comes easy, but in difficult times when the pages of life are turned and we feel that the odds are against us. And so "Dad" Land did on March 18, 1919 at Kansas City, Missouri set out to accomplish his vision.

JACQUES (DeMOLAI) DeMOLAY

"Dad" Land's Fraternal Order was patterned and actually named after Jacques DeMolay, the last Grand Master of the Medieval Crusaders who we know as the Knights Templar. The Knights Templar had participated fearlessly in numerous Crusades. The name of the Order was a byword for heroism. In 1297 Jacques DeMolay was elected Grand Master, an office that ranked him often times above great lords and princes of the era.

DeMolay became Grand Master at a time when the situation for Christianity in the East was in a precarious way. The infidel Saracens had defeated the Crusaders, and only the Knights Templar and the Hospitallers were left to confront them.

Philip the Fair, King of France, avid for the immense power he would have if he could Unite the Orders of Templar and Hospitallers with himself in control, set about to do so. Unsuccessful in his power-grab Philip actually persuaded and then joined with Pope Clement V, on a mission to destroy the Templars in order to prevent any rise in power of the Papacy, since the Orders were accountable only to the Church.

THE INTERNATIONAL SUPREME COUNCIL

The governing body of the Order of DeMolay, is the International Supreme Council, it is the Supreme authority in all matters pertaining to the governing of the Order. It regulates and has control over all laws, statutes, chapters, Advisory Councils, members, charters, finances, rituals, and officers. The purpose of the body is not only to establish regulations, which are for the protection, advancement and benefit of the organization, but also to see that the rulings are carried out and the Order benefited.

From an organizational posture the Supreme Council functions directly with each DeMolay Jurisdiction .DeMolay is divided into jurisdictions which may be either entire or parts of states, provinces, territories or countries, depending on their physical size. Each jurisdiction is supervised by an Active Member or Deputy of the Supreme Council who is known as the Executive Officer for that jurisdiction.

The Executive Officer is the official representative of the Supreme Council in all DeMolay affairs in each jurisdiction. He possesses and may exercise within his jurisdictions such powers and authority as may be necessary for the interest of the Order which are not prohibited by the Statutes, Order of the Supreme Council or the Grand Master.

The Executive Officer works closely with the Grand Secretary. The Grand Secretary is the chief administrative officer of the Supreme Council with the responsibility of extending and promoting the program of the Order of DeMolay in every jurisdiction and chapter. He employs a staff of dedicated people at DeMolay Headquarters in Kansas City to carry forth these responsibilities. DeMolay

Headquarters serves as the nerve center for the world-wide DeMolay operation under the direction of the Grand Secretary.

The International Supreme Council session is a four-day meeting held in a different DeMolay jurisdiction each year. Master Masons who are dedicated to the Order are selected as members of the Supreme Council.

HOW DeMOLAY FUNCTIONS

The real secret of how the Order of DeMolay functions can be found in the heart of the typical DeMolay volunteer who serves as an Advisor. These DeMolay "Dads" and now "Moms" are uniquely special in that they live the Masonic commitment of evidencing a desire to help good boys develop into better men.

No matter what the size of the jurisdiction involved, every Executive Officer, because he is a volunteer, is not going to have the time or the means to do everything he would like for DeMolay or be everywhere he should be in his jurisdiction. As a result, the executive officer and his Adjuant Dad Nick Auck seeks to appoint other interested and dedicated Masons to serve as his personal representatives and to help DeMolay in assigned geographic sections, or in specialty areas like ritual, public relations, or membership.

Next in the chain of command is the chapter itself. Every DeMolay chapter has a sponsor which must be either a recognized Masonic Organization such as a Lodge or Scottish Rite Valley or possibly fifteen individuals preferably Master Masons forming a group for the purpose of sponsoring a DeMolay chapter.

The sponsoring body passes a resolution of sponsorship, pledging itself to supervise, Guide, and assist a DeMolay chapter. Basically, the sponsoring body agrees to serve as Advisors to the chapter; to assist in providing a place for the chapter to meet; and to furnish not only interest in the chapter and its activities, but also to provide the moral discipline and ultimate responsibility of seeing that the chapter functions properly. The chapter will be just as strong as its Advisors, for the Advisors provide the experience, the continuity, and the personal example that the DeMolay membership need to run a chapter properly. Having the young men appreciate that they are uniquely special and to view life with anticipated discoveries and dreams molded by the DeMolay ideals.

Normally, each member of the Chapter Advisory Council will be assigned specific duties to assist the chapter, such as in the area of ritual, athletics, social affairs, civic affairs, finances and other similar categories. The Chapter Advisor is the principal member of the Advisory Council that serves as spokesman for the council to the DeMolays.

In a normal functioning chapter, the young men as officers and members actually run and administer the chapter functions and activities, with only the wise council and advise from the Advisors.

ADVISORS

Every De Molay chapter is supervised by a group of adult Advisors. These Advisors form an Advisory Council and each member of the council are preferred to be a Master Mason in good standing. However today in DeMolay it is not a requirement to be a Master Mason. An advisor can be known persons of interest which includes family members such as wives, mothers, aunts and grandmothers.

In view of the circumstances surrounding the founding of DeMolay and as "Dad", a very active Mason and employee of the Scottish Rite, the order began by holding the original group's meetings at the Scottish Rite Temple. As the founder was a Masonic Scholar, principally writing in the Ritual, it was only natural that DeMolay would be strongly tied to Masonry and look to the Masonic Fraternity for it's adult leadership however because of fewer committed advisors, the rules for advisors has been expanded.

In Louisiana each Advisory Council must consist of a minimum of fifteen preferably Master Masons. The sponsoring body of a chapter is responsible for recommending these Advisory Council members to the Supreme Council Deputy, the Executive Officer in charge of the jurisdiction. The Executive Officer then actually does the appointing or reappointing on a yearly basis.

The other key member on the council is the Chapter Advisor who is primary spokesman between the Chapter Advisory Council and the chapter members. All advisors have special titles of honor and are referred to as either "Dad" or "Mom" and the Chapter Advisor is referred to as "The Chapter Mom or Dad".

"Dad" and "Mom" Advisors are volunteers who give freely of their time and efforts because of the interest in the youth of their community. They become a confidant and councilor to the De Molay members as they journey through that difficult period of a young man's life known as adolescence, a time when a young man must face the reality of knowing he must fight his own battles but being assured that in his corner is his "Dad" advisor with a bucket and cold sponge. The young men come to realize that all the problems that are faced in adolescence can not be fixed but they learn that their mentors will always be there. The advisor as a mentor shows by example the fundamental value of human kind by caring for the DeMolays in his chapter, knowing full well that he is preparing his young men for a world that he will never know. The Chapter "Dad" or "Mom" will leave a legacy of character and loyalty that will last for generations, a legacy of caring that will touch each of their lives and each life over which each DeMolay will have influence.

The success of any DeMolay chapter relies, without question, more on these dedicated Advisors working with the chapter. If you have a dedicated caring, hard working Chapter Advisory Council, you will have a good chapter and outstanding DeMolays who will make society a better place.

We emphasize that the purpose of the Advisory Council is not to run the chapter for the boys, but rather to stand behind the scenes and let the DeMolay run their own chapter, with the Advisors counseling the boys only where needed in the event they stray too far from the path of proper chapter operations.

And what does the Advisor receive for all his hard work and efforts? Personal satisfaction and the warm pride of seeing "their boys" grow into manhood and take their place as the leaders in his city, state and nation, and of course hopefully, our Masonic Fraternity.

Are you looking for a dynamic commitment for your life, a life changing experience? An unselfish purpose that would further you Masonic search for light, a defined purpose that will give you the opportunity to positively influence and change the lives of the young men of your DeMolay Chapter. What you will find is that it will be an experience that will not only be a beacon for the youth, it will change your heart in a profound way. You do not have to look far. It is right before you. It is your Masonic Family and its Youth. Your purpose can be found in becoming an adviser to DeMolay. A life changing experience I herewith place in your hands.

If you are ready to adopt the spirit of Grand Master, Jacque DeMolay, please contact me at chipborne43@aol.com.

Recognition of a New Grand Lodge in France (1913)

by Alain Bernheim, 33°

IN 1973, Bro. Will Read read before *Quatuor Coronati* Lodge a paper about Sir Alfred Robbins who was appointed President of the Board of General Purposes on 4 June 1913. Read mentioned the meeting of Grand Lodge on the following 3 December and that 'there was to be a message from the Grand Master'[1] but did not show what that message said, which was this:

> It is with deep satisfaction that I find myself able to signalize the auspicious occasion of the Centenary of the Union by an announcement which will, I am convinced, cause true rejoicing throughout the Craft.
>
> A body of Freemasons in France, confronted by a positive prohibition on the part of the Grand Orient to work in the name of the Great Architect of the Universe have, in fidelity to their Masonic pledges, resolved to uphold the true principles and tenets of the Craft, and have united several Lodges as the Independent and Regular National Grand Lodge of France and of the French Colonies.

In the same paper, Will Read wrote:

> [...] in the nineteen-twenties, [...] many Grand Lodges desired therefore to be recognized by the United Grand Lodge. Each application was treated on its merits and examined against the customs, practices and principles followed within the English Craft; *but these had never been defined or codified*[2].

He added in a foot-note to the above sentence:

> Some of these principles were defined and listed as 'obligations' when recognition was accorded to the newly-formed 'Independent and Regular Grand Lodge of France and of the French Colonies'. (Title changed in 1948 to 'Grande Loge Nationale Française') vide *Grand Lodge Proceedings*, 1913, p. 78.

Bro. Read did not quote either the wording of these 'obligations' which were read before Grand Lodge the same day, 3 December 1913, by Lord Ampthill, MW Pro Grand Master[3]:

The obligations which will be imposed on all Lodges under this new Constitution are the following:

1. While the Lodge is at work the Bible will always be open on the altar.
2. The ceremonies will be conducted in strict conformity with the Ritual of the "Regime Rectifié" which is followed by these Lodges, a Ritual which was drawn up in 1778 and sanctioned in 1782, and with which the Duke of Kent was initiated in 1792[4].
3. The Lodge will always be opened and closed with invocation and in the name of the Great Architect of the Universe. All the summonses of the Order and of the Lodges will be printed with the symbols of the Great Architect of the Universe.
4. No religious or political discussion will be permitted in the Lodge.
5. The Lodge as such will never take part officially in any political affair but every individual Brother will preserve complete liberty of opinion and action.
6. Only those Brethren who are recognised as true Brethren by the Grand Lodge of England will be received in Lodge.

It may come as a surprise to many that the above 'Obligations' were the faithful translation of suggestions included in two letters written by Dr. de Ribaucourt to England and noways the result of a decision by the United Grand Lodge of England[5].

In spite of statements made by Ribaucourt in various letters he sent to England between 20 September and 13 November 1913 (the new Grand Lodge was to be composed of 'three lodges', 'at least five lodges', 'many lodges', 'sixty lodges decline to remain in the Grand Orient')[6], the new Grand Lodge was created on 5 November 1913 by one single lodge, *Le Centre des Amis*[7], founded three years earlier[8]. Edmond de Ribaucourt, Worshipful Master of the lodge, became the first Grand Master. His Grand Lodge was recognized by the United

Grand Lodge of England in a letter signed jointly on 20 November 1913 by Lord Ampthill and Sir Edward Letchworth:

> We were quite prepared to receive your letter from 8 October [...] [9]. We have full authority to act in the name of our G. M., H. R. H. the Duke of Connaught [...] and accordingly in the name of H. R. H. we are eager to assure you that the G.L.N.I. et R. is recognized by the G. L. of England as a sovereign G. L. with which we wish to establish and entertain brotherly relations[10].

Two weeks later, on 3 December[11], another lodge, *L'Anglaise No. 204*, demitted from the Grand Orient of France. The next day it joined the new Grand Lodge and somewhat later received its *Décret* N° 2 which said:

> Our Sovereign Grand Committee, in its meeting of 15 December 1913, decided to recognize your Very Worshipful Grand Lodge [*sic*] as being an integral part of our Obedience since 4 December 1913, the day of your official adhesion to our *Régime*[12].

Finally, the third lodge of the new Grand Lodge was consecrated on 20 June 1914[13].

-

'Those Basic Principles of Freemasonry *for which the Grand Lodge of England has stood throughout its history*' (my italics) – seldom quoted words which stay at the head of this well-known document – were accepted by Grand Lodge on 4 September 1929 (14). They requested:

> 1. Regularity of origin, i.e. each Grand Lodge shall have been established lawfully by a duly recognized Grand Lodge or by three or more regularly constituted Lodges.

In 1975, Bro. George Draffen retorted:
> The National Grand Lodge of France is often quoted as a Grand Lodge founded by only two (!) Lodges and accepted as regular, but this was in December 1913, i.e. sixteen years before the United Grand Lodge of England adopted the regulation stipulating a minimum of three. [...] Two old (!) French Lodges[15]

[...] were responsible for the formation of this new Grand Lodge [...] the fact that it had been formed by only two Lodges in no way invalidated this[16].

All this being taken under consideration, one is reminded of sensible remarks made by English scholars. One by Gould:

Of the Ancient Landmarks it has been observed, with more or less foundation of truth: "Nobody knows what they comprise or omit: they are of no earthly authority, because everything is a landmark when an opponent desires to silence you, but nothing is a landmark that stands in his own way." (*Freemasons' Magazine*, February 25, 1865, p. 139)[17].

The other by Knoop and Jones:

For good or evil the freemasonry of London and Westminster in the age of Walpole showed what are regarded as common British characteristics. [...] a reluctance or incapacity to follow an argument to its end, and a disposition to be satisfied with a somewhat illogical position[18].

APPENDIX 1

GRAND LODGE MEETING, 3 DECEMBER 1913

The Grand Secretary [Sir Edward Letchworth] read the following message[19] from the MW Grand Master [HRH Arthur, Duke of Connaught and Strathearn].

"It is with deep satisfaction that I find myself able to signalize the auspicious occasion of the Centenary of the Union by an announcement which will, I am convinced, cause true rejoicing throughout the Craft.

"A body of Freemasons in France, confronted by a positive prohibition on the part of the Grand Orient to work in the name of the Great Architect of the Universe have, in fidelity to their Masonic pledges, resolved to uphold the true principles and tenets of the Craft, and have united several Lodges as the Independent and Regular National Grand Lodge of France and of the French Colonies.

"This new body has approached me with the request that it may be recognised by the Grand Lodge of England and, having received full assurance that it is pledged to adhere to those principles of Freemasonry which we regard as fundamental and essential, I have joyfully assented to the establishment of fraternal relations and the exchange of representatives.

"We are thus enabled to celebrate the hundredth anniversary of that Union which was the foundation of our solidarity and world-wide influence, by the consummation of a wish which has been ardently cherished by English Freemasons for many years, and we are once more in the happy position of being able to enjoy Masonic intercourse with men of the great French nation.

"I trust that the bond thus established will strengthen and promote the good understanding which exists outside of the sphere of Freemasonry."

MW Pro Grand Master [Lord Ampthill].

Brethren, the happy announcement to which you have just listened has been made to you in the form of a Message from the Throne in conformity with precedent and in order to mark its great importance. You will, I am sure, not deem it inappropriate that I should add a few words of explanation.

The agreement with this newly constituted body of French Freemasons is the result of prolonged and difficult negotiations in which two well-known brethren have been devoted and skilful intermediaries. It is no more than their due to mention their names as they hold no official positions and have done their work, not as a matter of duty but from disinterested devotion to the Craft. They are Bro. Edward Roehrich (20), who plays so prominent a part in the work of the Anglo-foreign Lodges in London, and Bro. Frederick Crowe (21), to whose self-denial, no less than to the enterprise and generosity of other Brethren, we owe the proud possession of the valuable collection of documents which are now being displayed in the Library.

The Lodge in France which took the lead in withstanding the prohibition of the Grand Orient is the Lodge "Le Centre des Amis" of Paris, in which the guiding spirit has been Bro. Dr. De Ribaucourt.

Bro. de Ribaucourt has been elected Grand Master of the newly constituted Independent and Regular National Grand Lodge of France to which, we have good reason to expect, there will be many accessions of Lodges under this new Constitution all over France.

The obligations which will be imposed on all Lodges under this new Constitution are the following:

1)   While the Lodge is at work the Bible will always be open on the altar.

2)   The ceremonies will be conducted in strict conformity with the Ritual of the "Regime Rectifié" which is followed by these Lodges, a Ritual which was drawn up in 1778 and sanctioned in 1782, and with which the Duke of Kent was initiated in 1792.

3)   The Lodge will always be opened and closed with invocation and in the name of the Great Architect of the Universe. All the summonses of the Order and of the Lodges will be printed with the symbols of the Great Architect of the Universe.

4)   No religious or political discussion will be permitted in the Lodge.

5)   The Lodge as such will never take part officially in any political affair but every individual Brother will preserve complete liberty of opinion and action.

6)   Only those Brethren who are recognised as true Brethren by the Grand Lodge of England will be received in Lodge.

You will permit me, I am sure, to express my own deep satisfaction that the privation of Masonic intercourse with Frenchmen in France, which has for so long caused us so much sadness, is now at an end.

Now that there is a body of Frenchmen, a body which I do not doubt will grow very largely, who regard Freemasonry from the same point of view as we do, we can look forward to a most desirable extension of the principal work which lies before us, namely, that of promoting good understanding and goodwill between nations by the fraternal intercourse of individual men and culture.

I venture to think that no happier or more auspicious event could have coincided with the celebration of the Union which, effected a hundred years ago by the mutual goodwill and concession of men of truly Masonic spirit, has resulted in ever increasing prosperity and power.

APPENDIX 2

Alec Mellor (1907-1988), was made a Mason on 28 March 1969. In 1980 he issued a book, *La Grande Loge Nationale Française,* in which he states that the Board of General Purposes allowed him to reproduce specific letters from 1913 related to the creation of the new French Grand Lodge and thanked Sir James Stubbs and Terence Haunch for their brotherly reception (Mellor 1980, 245).

In 2011, thanks to the help provided by M. Martin Cherry, Librarian, and by Ms Susan A Snell, Archivist and Records Manager of the Library and Museum of Freemasonry at Freemasons' Hall, I was allowed to study folder HC 25 headed

> Folder contains bundle of letters from Lord Ampthill, Pro. G. Master to Sir Edward Letchworth, G. Secretary [of the Grand Lodge of England]. Letters are in French and English and are typed and handwritten.

Whoever prepared this folder[22] added the following remark: 'I have only given a paraphrased translation of the French letters here.'

Some letters included in folder HC 25 were not reproduced or mentioned in Mellor's book. The folder includes the original of Ribaucourt's letter to HRH the Duke of Connaught (mentioned above in foot-note 5). On the origial the word October is not crossed out but it is so on its facsimilé reproduction in Mellors book. Mellor commented: 'the 8 October date which stays at the end of the letter is a mistake. It was corrected into « 8 November 1913 » on page 1'.

This appears to be a conclusion of Mellor because in a letter sent by Ribaucourt to Roehrich on 9 October, Ribaucourt wrote: 'As soon as there will be an answer from London [...].[23] Further, the letter from 20 November 1913, signed jointly by Lord Ampthill and Sir Edward Letchworth, opens with the words: 'We were all prepared to receive your letter from 8 October'.[24]

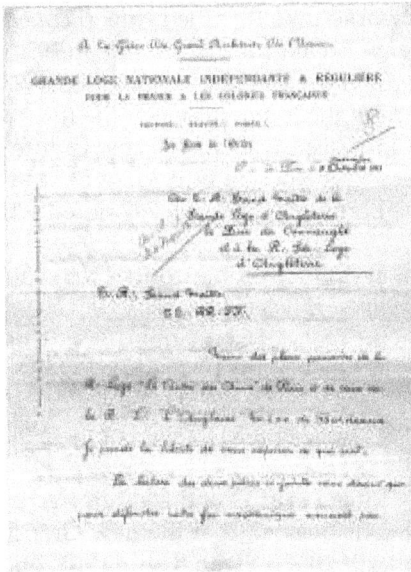

Left, the original document which is in the Library and Museum Historical Correspondence Box 25 in a slim folder marked (France – Historical Correspondence).

Right, the unnumbered page 269 of Alec Mellor's 1980 with the word October struck out.

NOTES

1. *AQC* 86 (1973), p. 105.
2. *AQC* 86 (1973), p. 114. My italics.
3. The message of HRH the Duke of Connaught and the allocution of Lord Ampthill are quoted in the Appendix.
4. Edward Augustus Hanover (2 November 1767-23 January 1820) was created 1st Duke of Kent on 24 April 1799 (*http://www.thepeerage.com/ p10078.htm#i100780*). HRH was initiated on 5 August 1789 (not 'in 1790', as stated pp. 120 & 235 of Grand Lodge 1717-1767) in the Geneva lodge *L'Union* (not *L'Union des Cœurs*, as stated ibid., p. 275). *L'Union* and *L'Union des Cœurs*

were two distinct Geneva lodges. *L'Union*, founded on 20 March 1786, was the lodge of the Grand Master of the *Grand Orient National de Genève*, Jean Rodolphe Sigismond Vernet, and never worked the Rectified Rite. *L'Union des Cœurs*, founded in 1769, joined the *Régime Rectifié* in 1810 (Bernheim 1994, pp. 303 & 539). The dates 1778 and 1782 are those of *Convents* held in Lyon and in Wilhemsbad. The mistake concerning the lodge in which the future Duke of Kent was initiated, originated in three Swiss historians, Galiffe, Zschokke and Boos; it was set right by François Ruchon in 1935, quoted by Paul Tunbridge (AQC 78, 1965, p. 19). See Bernheim 1994, pp. 247 note 13 & 303 note 27.

5. '*Voici les engagements que nous pouvons prendre*' in Ribaucourt's letter to Roehrich, 17 September 1913. '*Nous avons imposé et nous imposerons à nos Loges les obligations suivantes*' in his letter to HRH the Duke of Connaught, 8 October November 1913 (facsimiles of both letters in Alec Mellor 1980, pp. 247-248 & 269-[273].

6. From the seventeen letters in Mellor 1980, pp. 247-[281], seven of them as fac-similés. But see Appendix 2.

7. Dated 6 December 1913 and signed by Ribaucourt Grand Master, *Décret N° 1* of the new Grand Lodge said: '[...] considering: That the new Grand Lodge was founded in Paris on 5 November 1913 [...]' (Jean Baylot 1963, pp. 27-28, and Alec Mellor 1980, p. 90). Twenty years ago, I mentioned that this Grand Lodge was founded by one lodge only, AQC 101 (1989), p. 98.

8. *Le Centre des Amis* was the new name adopted in 1793 by lodge *Guillaume Tell*. It lapsed in 1841 (*Adhuc Stat*, p. 15). Three members of the Grand Orient (Édouard de Ribaucourt was one of them) who received the *Chevalier Bienfaisante de la Cité Sainte* (CBCS) degree in Geneva on 11 June 1910 created an unattached lodge working the Rectified Rite under the name *Le Centre des Amis* in Paris on the following 20 June. In a letter they sent in July to the Grand Orient of France, they asserted to have 're-awakened that lodge in virtue of a constitutive patent dated 11 June 1910, delivered to them by the *Directoire du Régime Écossais Rectifié en Helvétie* (Charrière 1938, p. 98). After a rebuke for its illegal action, the lodge was warranted by the Grand Orient on 15 March 1911 (ibid., p. 108).

9. In view of these words, it is noteworthy that in the letter to HRH the Duke of Connaught, mentioned above (footnote 5), the word *Octobre* is struck out in the facsimilé reproduction in Mellor's book and the word *Novembre* written above it (see Appendix 2).

10. The above is my re-translation of the French text quoted in Jean Baylot 1963, pp. 34-35 & Alec Mellor 1980, pp. 86-87: '*Nous étions tout préparés à recevoir votre Pl. du 8 octobre* [...] *Nous avons toute autorité pour agir au nom de notre G.M., S.A.R. le Duc de Connaught* [...] *et au nom de S.A.R. nous nous empressons de vous donner l'assurance que la G.L.N.I. et R. est de ce fait reconnue par la G.L. d'Angleterre comme une G.L. souveraine avec laquelle nous désirons établir et entretenir des relations fraternelles.*'

11. According to the history of the lodge on its website *http://www.anglaise204.org/page44.html* and to the first history of the lodge written in 1915 by Bro. Renou (a typescript I found in the library of UGLE [ref. 4FR 166 (204) REN], pp. 30-32). On page 32, Renou writes that on 3 December 1913, the lodge was closed for the last time in the name and under the auspices of the Grand Orient of France.

12. Jean Baylot 1963, p. 28. The words 'our *Régime*' mean the Rectified Rite.

13. Jean Baylot 1963, pp. 37 & 89.

14. Quoted in *Masonic Year Books* as well as in Appendix B of Bro. James Daniel's paper, *AQC* 120 (2005), p. 41. My italics.

15. Lodge *Le Centre des Amis* was founded in 1910 (see note 8).

16. *AQC* 88 (1976), p. 85. A few years later, Draffen wrote: 'All help should be given to see that the new Grand Lodges do not stray into the enemy's camp and become one of those Grand Lodges dominated by the thinking of the Grand Orient of France', *AQC* 96 (1984), p. 135.

17. R.F. Gould 1882-1887, *The History of Freemasonry*, Vol. I, p. 439, note 1.

18. Douglas Knoop and G.P. Jones, *AQC* 56 (1945), p. 47.

19. William Preston Campbell-Everden 1962. Freemasonry and its Etiquette, pp. 16-18.

20. [Note by AB]. 'Worshipful Brother Edward Roehrich was born in Geneva. [...] Founder, Past Master (twice W.M.) and Father of the Entente Cordiale Lodge, No. 2796, consecrated in London in 1899, and working entirely in the French language ; [...] In 1901 he was invested as Deputy Grand Director of Ceremonies of England, [...]. At the Grand Lodge of England he represents the Grande Loge Nationale of France, of which he is Past Senior Grand Warden. [...] It was chiefly through his advocacy and assistance that the National Grand Lodge of France was recently organised, whereby a severance between English and French Freemasons of nearly forty years was bridged over ; [...] At the Grand Lodge of England he acts as representative of the Grand Lodge Alpina (Switzerland)'. ([Anon.] 1915. *Representative British Freemasons - A Series of Biographies and Portraits of Early Twentieth Century Freemasons*. Kessinger reprint 2003, p. 216).

21. [Note by AB]. The reviser of R.F. Gould's *Concise History of Freemasonry* (1920).

22. Ms Snell wrote to me on 18 March 2011 : 'Two years ago we were fortunate in having an archive student on work experience here with excellent French skills. She provided us with text interpretations for the correspondence relating to events in 1913 of the letters to be found in the folder in HC 25. [...]We will be able to provide access to the originals when you visit us on 12 May.'

23. Mellor, p. 253.

24. The full text of that letter is translated in [anon. = Baylot 1963], p. 34 & Mellor, pp. 86-87.

BIBLIOGRAPHY OF FOREIGN QUOTED SOURCES

[anon.] *Adhuc Stat 1913-1963*. 1963. The two parts of this small booklet of 24 pages are signed *Petrus, Eques a Cygno* on p. 20 and A. V. on p. 23. It was printed in 1963 and described on p. 1 as 'Numéro spécial du Bulletin intérieur de la GLNF pour la commémoration de son cinquantième anniversaire'. This GLNF (Grande Loge Nationale Française) was the breakaway Grand Lodge which was founded in 1958 and had its head office 5 avenue de l'Opéra in Paris.]

[anon. = Jean Baylot] 1963. *Histoire de la Grande Loge Nationale Française 1913-1963*. Paris.

Alain Bernheim. 1974. *Les Débuts de la Franc-Maçonnerie à Genève et en Suisse*. Genève: Slatkine.

Louis Charrière. 1938. *Le Régime Écossais Rectifié et le Grand Orient de France*. En vente chez l'auteur: 15, rue Daubenton. Paris.

Alec Mellor. 1980. *La Grande Loge Nationale Française*. Paris: Belfond.

Reading Masons and Masons Who Do Not Read

by Albert G. Mackey, 33°

I SUPPOSE there are more Masons who are ignorant of all the principles of freemasonry than there are men of any other class who are chargeable with the like ignorance of their own profession. There is not a watchmaker who does not know something about the elements of horology, nor is there a blacksmith who is altogether unacquainted with the properties of red-hot iron. Ascending to the higher walks of science, we would be much astonished to meet with a lawyer who was ignorant of the elements of jurisprudence, or a physician who had never read a treatise on pathology, or a clergyman who knew nothing whatever of theology. Nevertheless, nothing is more common than to encounter Freemasons who are in utter darkness as to every thing that relates to Freemasonry. They are ignorant of its history - they know not whether it is a mushroom production of today, or whether it goes back to remote ages for its origin. They have no comprehension of the esoteric meaning of its symbols or its ceremonies, and are hardly at home in its modes of recognition. And yet nothing is more common than to find such socialists in the possession of high degrees and sometimes honored with elevated affairs in the Order, present at the meetings of lodges and chapters, intermeddling with the proceedings, taking an active part in all discussions and pertinaciously maintaining heterodox opinions in opposition to the judgment of brethren of far greater knowledge.

Why, it may well be asked, should such things be? Why, in Masonry alone, should there be so much ignorance and so much presumption? If I ask a cobbler to make me a pair of boots, he tells me that he only mends and patches, and that he has not learned the higher branches of his craft, and then he honestly declines the offered job. If I request a watchmaker to construct a mainspring for my chronometer, he answers that he cannot do it, that he has never learned how to make mainsprings, which belongs to a higher branch of the business, but that if I will bring him a spring ready made, he will insert it in my timepiece, because that he knows how to do. If I go to an artist with an order to paint me a historical picture, he will tell me that it is beyond his capacity, that he has never studied nor practiced the compotation of details, but has confined himself to the painting of portraits. Were he dishonest and presumptuous he would take my order and instead of a picture give me a daub. It is the Freemason alone who wants this modesty. He is too apt to think that the obligation not only makes him a Mason, but a learned Mason at the same time. He too often imagines that the mystical ceremonies which induct him into the Order are all that are necessary to make him cognizant of its principles. There are some Christian sects who believe that the water of baptism at once washes away all sin, past and prospective. So there are some Masons who think that the mere act of initiation is at once followed by an influx of all Masonic knowledge. They need no further study or research. All that they require to know has already been received by a sort of intuitive process.

The great body of Masons may be divided into three classes. The first consists of those who made their application for initiation not from a desire for knowledge, but from some accidental motive, not always honorable. Such men have been led to seek reception either because it was likely, in their opinion, to facilitate their business operations, or to advance their political prospects, or in some other way to personally benefit them. In the commencement of a war, hundreds flock to the lodges in the hope of obtaining the "mystic sign," which will be of service in the hour of danger. Their object having been attained, or having failed to attain it, these men become indifferent and, in time, fall into the rank of the non-affiliates. Of such Masons there is no hope. They are dead trees having no promise of fruit. Let them pass as utterly worthless, and incapable of improvement.

There is a second class consisting of men who are the moral and Masonic antipodes of the first. These make their application for admission, being prompted, as the ritual requires, "by a favorable opinion conceived of the Institution, and a desire of knowledge." As soon as they are initiated, they see in the ceremonies through which they have passed a philosophical meaning worthy of the trouble of inquiry. They devote themselves to this inquiry. They obtain Masonic books, they read Masonic periodicals, and they converse with well-informed brethren. They make themselves acquainted with the history of the Association. They investigate its origin and its ultimate design. They explore the hidden sense of its symbols and they acquire the interpretation. Such Masons are always useful and honorable members of the Order, and very frequently they become its shining lights. Their lamp burns for the enlightenment of others, and to them the Institution is indebted for whatever of an elevated position it has attained. For them, this article is not written.

But between these two classes, just described, there is an intermediate one; not as bad as the first, but far below the second, which, unfortunately, comprises the body of the Fraternity.

This third class consists of Masons who joined the Society with unobjectionable motives, and with, perhaps the best intentions. But they have failed to carry these intentions into effect.

They have made a grievous mistake. They have supposed that initiation was all that was requisite to make them Masons, and that any further study was entirely unnecessary. Hence, they never read a Masonic book. Bring to their notice the productions of the most celebrated Masonic authors, and their remark is that they have no time to read-the claims of business are overwhelming. Show them a Masonic journal of recognized reputation, and ask them to subscribe. Their answer is that they cannot afford it, the times are hard and money is scarce.

And yet, there is no want of Masonic ambition in many of these men. But their ambition is not in the right direction. They have no thirst for knowledge, but they have a very great thirst for office or for degrees. They cannot afford money or time for the purchase or perusal of Masonic books, but they have enough of both to expend on the acquisition of Masonic degrees.

It is astonishing with what avidity some Masons who do not understand the simplest rudiments of their art, and who have utterly failed to comprehend the scope and meaning of primary, symbolic Masonry, grasp at the empty honors of the high degrees. The Master Mason who knows very little, if anything, of the Apprentice's degree longs to be a Knight Templar. He knows nothing, and never expects to know anything, of the history of Templarism, or how and why these old crusaders became incorporated with the Masonic brotherhood. The height of his ambition is to wear the Templar cross upon his breast. If he has entered the Scottish Rite, the Lodge of Perfection will not content him, although it supplies material for months of study. He would fain rise higher in the scale of rank, and if by persevering efforts he can attain the summit of the Rite and be invested with the Thirty-third degree, little cares he for any knowledge of the organization of the Rite or the sublime lessons that it teaches. He has reached the height of his ambition and is permitted to wear the double-headed eagle.

Such Masons are distinguished not by the amount of knowledge that they possess, but by the number of the jewels that they wear. They will give fifty dollars for a decoration, but not fifty cents for a book.

These men do great injury to Masonry. They have been called its drones. But they are more than that. They are the wasps, the deadly enemy of the industrious bees. They set a bad example to the younger Masons - they discourage the growth of Masonic literature - they drive intellectual men, who would be willing to cultivate Masonic science, into other fields of labor - they depress the energies of our writers - and they debase the character of Speculative Masonry as a branch of mental and moral philosophy. When outsiders see men holding high rank and office in the Order who are almost as ignorant as themselves of the principles of Freemasonry, and who, if asked, would say they looked upon it only as a social institution, these outsiders very naturally conclude that there cannot be anything of great value in a system whose highest positions are held by men who profess to have no knowledge of its higher development.

It must not be supposed that every Mason is expected to be a learned Mason, or that every man who is initiated is required to devote himself to the study of Masonic science and literature. Such an expectation would be foolish and unreasonable. All men are not equally competent to grasp and retain the same amount of knowledge. Order, says Pope-Order is heaven's first law and this confess, some are, and must be, greater than the rest, richer, wiser.

All that I contend for is that when a candidate enters the fold of Masonry he should feel that there is something in it better than its mere grips and signs, and that he should endeavor with all his ability to attain some knowledge of that better thing. He should not seek advancement to higher degrees until he knew something of the lower, nor grasp at office, unless he had previously fulfilled with some reputation for Masonic knowledge, the duties of a private station. I once knew a brother whose greed for office led him to pass through all the grades from Warden of his lodge to Grand Master of the jurisdiction, and who during that whole period had never read a Masonic book nor attempted to comprehend the meaning of a single symbol. For the year of his Mastership he always found it convenient to have an excuse for absence from the lodge on the nights when degrees were to be conferred. Yet, by his personal and social influences, he had succeeded in elevating himself in rank above all those who were above him in Masonic knowledge. They were really far above him, for they all knew something, and he knew nothing. Had he remained in the background, none could have complained. But, being where he was, and seeking himself the position, he had no right to be ignorant. It was his presumption that constituted his offense.

A more striking example is the following: A few years ago while editing a Masonic periodical; I received a letter from the Grand Lecturer of a certain Grand Lodge who had been a subscriber, but who desired to discontinue his subscription. In assigning his reason, he said (a copy of the letter is now before me), "although the work contains much valuable information, I shall have no time to read, as I shall devote the whole of the present year to teaching." I cannot but imagine what a teacher such a man must have been, and what pupils he must have instructed.

This article is longer than I intended it to be. But I feel the importance of the subject. There are in the United States more than four hundred thousand affiliated Masons. How many of these are readers? One-half - or even one-tenth? If only one-fourth of the men who are in the Order would read a little about it, and not depend for all they know of it on their visits to their lodges, they would entertain more elevated notions of its character. Through their sympathy scholars would be encouraged to discuss its principles and to give to the public the results of their thoughts, and good Masonic magazines would enjoy a prosperous existence.

Now, because there are so few Masons that read, Masonic books hardly do more than pay the publishers the expense of printing, while the authors get nothing; and Masonic journals are being year after year carried off into the literary Academia, where the corpses of defunct periodicals are deposited; and, worst of all, Masonry endures depressing blows.

The Mason, who reads, however little, is it only the pages of the monthly magazine to which he subscribes, will entertain higher views of the Institution and enjoy new delights in the possession of these views. The Masons who do not read will know nothing of the interior beauties of Speculative Masonry, but will be content to suppose it to be something like Odd Fellowship, or the Order of the Knights of Pythias - only, perhaps, a little older. Such a Mason must be an indifferent one. He has laid no foundation for zeal.

If this indifference, instead of being checked, becomes more widely spread, the result is too apparent. Freemasonry must step down from the elevated position which she has been struggling, through the efforts of her scholars, to maintain, and our lodges, instead of becoming resorts for speculative and philosophical thought, will deteriorate into social clubs or mere benefit societies. With so many rivals in that field, her struggle for a prosperous life will be a hard one.

The ultimate success of Masonry depends on the intelligence of her disciples.

The Chamber of Reflection

by Michael Carpenter, PM
Presented at the Scottish Rite Bicentennial Academic Symposium - June 1, 2, 3, and 4, 2011. New Orleans, LA

> *After crossing the threshold I found myself facing the question posed to every man, but one which the profane world turns away from: the testament which was asked of me and the skull whose empty eyes were focused on me, questioning my degree of awareness [of] the ineluctable completion of all destinies.[1]*

IF YOU were initiated in a Scottish or French Rite blue lodge, you would have experienced a stay in the Chamber of Reflection. You would have had to meditate on why you wanted to become a Mason and write an ethical or philosophical last will and testament in a somber and melancholy environment, having been left in solitude for some lengthy time. This Chamber of Reflection, or *Cabinet de réflexion*, is a French contribution to Freemasonry, which originated, it appears, in the French Rite, and then was adopted in the Scottish Rite system of blue lodge degrees. In this presentation, I'm going to discuss only the chamber which appears in the blue lodge, and not any which may appear in the so-called *hauts grades*. In today's speech, virtually all the material I will discuss is French in origin, with the exception of Albert Pike's rendition of the Scottish Rite version of a ritual for the first three degrees, and Pike's description is only a how-to-build-it for a hypothetical blue lodge system under the control of a Scottish Rite Supreme Council.

Since very few Americans start their Masonic journeys in a Chamber of Reflection, and a significant number of the rest of us haven't even seen one, and, if they have, they haven't had the opportunity to look at it in detail, it would be best to describe it before discussing what the candidate is supposed to experience within it and how that experience provides the initiation ceremony with additional meaning. I shall proceed by first describing hypotheses about the development of Chambers of Reflection and, secondly, I shall discuss their symbolism and use, material which I hope will cause some discussion.

Development of the Chamber of Reflection: History and Hypotheses: When Masonry came to France in the 1730s, it was the Masonry of the Moderns that was practiced because the Antients had yet to develop. Shortly before Masonry was introduced into France, the premier Grand Lodge implemented ritual changes in order to deal with Samuel Prichard's exposure, *Masonry Dissected*. The French still maintain those changes, at least within the French Rite in spite of the 1816 ritual compromises occasioned by the 1813 union of the Antients and Moderns in England, compromises which sealed the English groups revocation of the changes. And France had (and has) a culture different from that of England. Rituals in France became increasingly spectacular. New degrees came into existence. Now called *écossais* (French for 'Scottish'), these "higher degrees" provided a way for the French nobility to emphasize their social distinctions. So it was that the French lodges had a greater percentage of upper class brothers than did those in England.[2]

One of the French innovations, so it has seemed to many Masonic historians, is the Chamber of Reflection (*Cabinet de réflexion*). Perhaps first noticed in a French exposure of 1745, the Abbé Gabriel-Louis Pérau's anonymously published *Le secret des francs-maçons* contains a description of a darkened room in which the candidate is deprived of all metals, something, except for the darkening, best resembling a preparation room.[3]

Moving on to the year 1765, we find a description of something now called a Chamber of Reflection in a ritual from the first Grand Lodge of France, an organization that would later become the Grand Orient. Here is the description from that ritual:

> *Apartment of Brother Terrible.* No matter that this apartment has no particular design—it can be purely arbitrary, it is nevertheless proper that it have a gloomy and dismal appearance and convey rather more than less horror, [at least] according to the way the Candidate will perceive it; it can be draped in black, with a lamp giving off but a weak light. Again, it can have a dungeon door with a bolt and chains. Brother Terrible must be under a black mantle seated beside a table or prie-dieu on which there will be a white kerchief and a sword. [Nothing further is stated of the conditions or actions in the room][4]

Yet, these, and other references I have not summarized here, fail to provide a clear difference between a Chamber of Reflection and a preparation room. The first adequate description I've found of a Chamber of Reflection, as distinct from the preparation room, is found in Ex-Vén's 1788 *Recueil des trois premiers grades de la Maçonnerie sous la dénomination d'apprenti, compagnon et maître,* some forty-three years later than Pérau. Here is the description:

> This room must be closed off from the rays of the day, lit with a single lamp, the walls will be blackened and decorated with funereal ornaments in order to inspire meditation, sadness, and fright: phrases of pure morality, maxims of austere philosophy will be written legibly on the walls, or framed and hung in divers places in the room: a skull & even a skeleton, if one can be procured, recalling the nothingness of human affairs.

> In this room there must be no more than a chair, a table, a vase filled with clear water, salt and sulfur in two small vases, a book of piety, some paper, some pens & ink. Above the table will be represented a cock & an hourglass and at the bottom of these emblems will be these words: *Vigilance & Perseverance.*[5]

The maxims and phrases on the wall are consistent with, if not the origin, of those I'll discuss near the end of this paper, with the exception of the following phrase which is clearly based on alchemy: If you persevere, you will be purified by the elements, you will leave the abyss of shadows and you will see the light.[6]

With this bit of material, it would appear that the Chamber of Reflection came from France. However, aside from hints in a few early English exposures, we don't really know what constituted the ritual for the Moderns in England. Could the Moderns too have had some sort of Chamber of Reflection, a feature which was removed, along with so much else from the English ritual in the 1813-1816 period? Lest this idea sound strange, we know from certain features found in almost every American ritual that a number of symbols disappeared from the English ritual, especially in the second and third degrees, matters on which I cannot touch here. In fact, many American rituals are older than the 1816 English ritual and its various workings.

Patrick Négrier, a former member of a lodge under the Grand Lodge of France, has written several books on Masonic history, among which are *Temple de Salomon et diagrammes symboliques : iconologie des tableaux de loge et du cabinet de réflexion* [The Temple of Solomon and Symbol Diagrams : Iconography of the Tracing Boards and the Chamber of Reflection], and *La Tulip : histoire du rite du Mot de maçon de 1637 à 1730* [The T.U.L.I.P.:[7] History of the Rite of the Mason Word, 1637-1730].[8] In these books Négrier re-examines early English and Scottish documents, finding them to contain what may be descriptions of a Chamber of Reflection long before the Grand Lodge era.

Négrier discusses a possible history, well prior to the 1742 Pérau exposure I described earlier, more ancient than we ever knew for the Chamber of Reflection. Négrier notes that in the Edinburgh Register House manuscript of 1696 the new candidate, when he first comes to the lodge is to be handled roughly and placed in a dark room with nothing in it in order to meditate on his condition and determine what he really wants to do with his life. When we get to the Dumfries no. 4 manuscript of ca. 1710, a death's head is shown or somehow presented to the candidate to become aware of his mortality.[9]

In his T.U.L.I.P. book, Négrier attempts to show that the two-degree system that existed prior to the premier grand lodge was based on a reification of the Mason Word as a result of the mixture of Scottish Calvinist and English Anglican approaches to the masons' guild and should be regarded as much a rite as the Scottish, York, and other ritual systems for the blue lodge degrees are. Although the details of his thesis iare beyond the scope of this paper, Négrier uses his claim to explain some of the contents of the Chamber of Reflection, especially in an effort to remove the aura of alchemy and occultism surrounding it.

To sum up this brief history of the Chamber of Reflection, we should note that the change from fear alone to a combination of meditation and fear, is but an illustration of the historical phenomenon that while the form remains the same, the meaning will change, just as the Fraternity has changed while its essence remains.

Now I must turn to the topic of just what a Chamber of Reflection is and what it contains.

Description of Chambers of Reflection: Options and Requisites: We will use the rudimentary description of a Chamber of Reflection as given in the 1788 French Rite ritual which will stand as a basis for further discussion. The late Daniel Béresniak provides an exhaustive list of the items likely to be found in a Chamber of Reflection in his monograph, *Le cabinet de réflexion : la demarche initiatique, technique de l'eveil* [10] and in chapter 2 of his *Rites et symbols de la Franc-maçonnerie, tome I: les loges bleues* [11]. Béresniak's list follows, although in an order other than his to facilitate the exposition:

- The will and testament. The last will and testament should be an ethical or moral testament, not a disposal of property, though this distinction is not always afforded the candidate. When complete the paper is often delivered to the master of the lodge at the end of a sword. Some forms ask the candidate to answer not the usual three but rather four questions before the candidate preparing his will and testament:

  1. What does man owe to God?
  2. What does he owe to himself?
  3. What does he owe to his fellow beings?
  4. What does he owe to his country?

Béresniak suggests that the last of these questions should not be asked of the candidate because Masonry acts on a different, non-temporal plane as distinguished from a political entity. In her best-selling *La symbolique maçonnique du troisième millénaire*, Irène Mainguy suggests that the last will and testament should be required, using a different fourth question: Were you at the hour of your death, tell us what the content of you philosophical testament would be (p. 180).[12]

- A Skull (and/or skeleton) The Chamber of Reflection of some lodges contains a skeleton standing in a dull black coffin. Others use only a clay skull. That a skull or other *memento mori* should be in front of the candidate in order to remind him of his own mortality seems reasonable in an environment in which a new man, a Mason, is about to be born as the result of the metaphorical death of the less enlightened person he is before initiation.

Mainguy classifies the symbols of the testament and the skull (and bones) as intellectual symbols; they refer to phenomena we can only meditate upon. The next, a double symbol, is physical in nature:

- Bread and Water. Bread and water are the minimum nourishment that we must have to live, so a piece of bread and a vase of water are on the table. These items are not to be found in every chamber of reflection; that they have a symbolic significance in light of their minimal nature of sustaining life, and thus provide suitable subjects for thought is not to be denied. Water is, of course, also the symbol for washing away our impurities.

The next class of symbols is temporal in nature, the hourglass and the scythe.

- The Hourglass denotes the passage of time and our inability to reverse its flow; what is done is done.

- The Scythe, a traditional emblem of death, not only to the stands of wheat that it is used to harvest, but also for each succeeding generation of humans whose time has come for the final harvest.

- The Hermetic Symbols (Salt, Sulfur (occasionally Mercury) as well as the Cock or Rooster) are probably the most difficult for any candidate to contemplate.

  1. Salt and sulfur (and mercury). According to numerous sources, salt and sulfur were first considered by alchemists as the two primary elements out of which all other compounds were to be derived. In the context of a Chamber of Reflection, these two are always to be present, or if not available, then the alchemical symbols for them, *viz.*

6 (Sulfur) 7 (Salt)

Now, why salt and sulfur? Négrier wants us to contemplate the destruction of Sodom as described in the Book of Genesis—sulfur poured down from the sky and destroyed the city; the wife of Lot, supposedly the only righteous man left in the city, turned into a pillar of salt. So these two elements would indicate the power of destruction to all things, especially to those who are not righteous. So, on Négrier's account, we would have divine destruction as the basis for the two elements rather than the primitive sources of generation. If Masonry was based on a Scottish Calvinistic view, as Négrier suggests, his suggestion makes sense. Of course, one must remember that there is more than one tradition of interpretation for why God destroyed Sodom, Gomorrah and a few other cities. And, if this version of the Cabinet of Reflection traveled to France, an alchemical interpretation could have come about in lieu of that originating from the wrath of God. Such changes of interpretation through time are common in Masonic history, just as they are in religious, political and social history.

By the time the ritual of the Chamber of Reflection, as hypothesized by Négrier, would have reached France, another theory of the fundamental alchemical elements would have developed, namely that of providing for three, rather than two, primal elements; salt and sulfur would now be joined by mercury, the new theory's First Matter from which all other elements are generated, especially with the aid of sulfur. The new alchemical explanation would have trumped the Biblical.

8(Mercury)

2. Cock or rooster. Because the cock or rooster announces the first light, he becomes a symbol of the return to clarity, according to Mainguy (p. 184). He is also the symbol of strength and courage for

fighting ignorance, subduing the passions, prejudice, error and hypocrisy, in short for mastering the impulses of the lower instincts (p. 184-85). All these virtues are why the cock is to be shown with the motto underneath him: Vigilance and Perseverance.

3. The Mottos on the Wall: Once the candidate has entered the Chamber of Reflection and removed his blindfold, and his eyes have adjusted to the low light, he will see the mottos that have been written on the wall or framed and hung on the wall. Although the symbols are supposed to reach him on an emotional level, and are thus subject, as all symbols should be, to multiple and developing interpretations, the written words on the walls of the chamber should communicate to him in a more direct fashion. Here are three of the mottos taken from the description of an idealized Chamber of Reflection as provided by Albert Pike:(13)

*   If mere curiosity brings you here, turn back; begone!
*   He that has no rule over his own spirit is a city dilapidated and without walls, and, interestingly,
*   The Glory of God is to conceal the Word.

These mottos are all readily intelligible. However, the following poster, while most often required in French Chambers of Reflection as well as some in the United States, is not readily intelligible because of its alchemical nature:

V.I.T.R.I.O.L.
(Visita interiora terrae. Rectificando, invenies occultum lapidum)

(Visit the interior of the Earth. While purifying yourself, you will find the Hidden Stone (i.e., the Hidden Truth))(14)

What do the mysterious letters V.I.T.R.I.O.L. mean? Were it not for the abbreviating periods, the word would simply be "vitriol," the old name for fuming sulfuric acid; the candidate might gather that, since vitriol is something that easily dissolves flesh and bone, link that idea to the fugitive nature of life, and even cause him to flee the lodge building for fear, not only of losing his life, but of having his body disappear in the bargain! (15) Or else, he could believe the word was being used in its figurative meaning and believe that the lodge members were impossibly angry with him. Another good reason to flee! Instead it is but an old alchemical motto.

A significant question is, if the V.I.T.R.I.O.L. poster is unintelligible to the candidate, and it means nothing to him, why have it? First, the symbols the candidate has seen in the chamber will all again appear before the candidate again, perhaps in different guises and surroundings, in the degrees which will follow should he proceed to receive all that is available in either the Scottish and/or French rites. By entering the Chamber of Reflection, the candidate will have received a preview of many of the Masonic symbols, symbols whose meaning he cannot yet discern.

Second, let me propose that although the Chamber of Reflection descends from French sources in which the Scottish and French Rites developed, Mainguy's suggestion that the Chamber of Reflection is not suitable for ritual regimes or rites descending from English ("Anglo-Saxon" to use her terminology) because of its alchemical sources is mistaken. Instead, not all the symbols and events in the Chamber of Reflection require alchemical sources; the mottos on the wall of the darkened room, the presence of emblems of mortality, even the bread and water, the hourglass and scythe are sufficient unto themselves to impress the candidate that he is about to undertake a significant change in his life. Isn't this the impression an initiatory ceremony should express in dramatic form? This line of thinking may be the reason that grand lodges of several states other than Louisiana have now allowed the use of a Chamber of Reflection. *Vive le cabinet de réflexion!*

NOTES

1. Fontaine, Pierre. "Impressions d'initiation (reconstitution du texte lu en loge on 1956)" in his *Sous la loi du silence : essais pour rendre la franc-maçonnerie intelligible aux hommes et aux femmes du XXIe siècle.* (Paris : Editions Véga, 2001), p. 16.

2. Since several Louisiana lodges held their first charters from the Grand Orient of France before the formation in 1812 of the Grand Lodge of Louisiana, and the established ritual of the time for the Grand Orient was the French Rite, I believe it most probable that this particular ritual was followed in the New Orleans French-speaking lodges, at least in the last decade of the eighteenth century through at least 1828, the date of publication for the *Manuel maçonnique*. See especially: Ancien Vénérable. *Manuel maçonnique, à l'usage des franc-maçons [sic] acceptés du Rite ancien d'York résidants à la Louisiane* (Nouvelle-Orléans : de l'Imprimerie d'Edwin Lyman, 1828), pp. 148-180. Copy in Special Collections, Louisiana State University Library.

3. [Pérau, Gabriel Louis]. *L'ordre des francs-maçons trahi, et Le secret des Mopses révélé* (Amsterdam, 1745. Reprint : Genève-Paris : Slatkine Reprints, 1980), p. 33.

4. *Corps complet de Maçonnerie adopté par la R.G.L. de France* [1765 ?], p. 9-10, in Mollier, Pierre (ed.) *Le régulateur du maçon 1785/"1801" : la fixation des grades symboliques du Rite français : histoire et documents*. Mémorable. (Paris : À l'Orient, 2004), pp. 241-242.

5. Ex-Vén. *Recueil des trois premiers grades de la Maçonnerie sous la dénomination d'apprenti, compagnon et maître* [Collection of the Three First Degrees of Freemasonry Called Apprentice, Fellow-Craft and Master] (À l'Orient de l'univers [i.e., Paris] : Entre l'équerre et le compas, 1788 ; reprint : Paris : À l'Orient, 2001). "Ex-Vble" stands for "former Vénérable" or "Past Worshipful Master." A slightly later description of the French Rite Chamber of Reflection can be found in: *Le régulateur du maçon*, Hérédon, 5801, in Mollier, Pierre (ed.) *Le régulateur du maçon*, p. 124.

6. Ex-Ven. *Recueil*, p. 8-10.

7. i.e. Total depravity, Unconditional election, Limited atonement, Irresistible grace, Perseverance of the saints. This is clearly a Calvinistic list, and, according to Négrier, Scottish Calvinism had a strong influence on Scottish Masonry.

8. Négrier, Patrick. *Temple de Salomon et diagrammes symboliques : iconologie des tableaux de loge et du cabinet de réflexion* (Grolay, France : Ivoire-claire, 2004) [The Temple of Solomon and Symbol Diagrams : Iconography of the Tracing Boards and the Chamber of Reflection], and *La Tulip : histoire du rite du Mot de maçon de 1637 à 1730* (Grolay, France : Ivoir-claire, 2005) [The T.U.L.I.P.: History of the Rite of the Mason Word, 1637-1730].

9. Two compilations which include transcriptions of the manuscript material are 1. *The Early Masonic Catechisms*, transcribed and edited by Douglas Knoop, G.P. Jones and Douglas Hamer. 2nd ed. by Hary Carr. (London : Quatuor Coronati Lodge, No. 2076, 1975), and *Les textes fondateurs de la franc-maçonnerie*, présentation, traduction commentaires de Philippe Langlet, t. 1 (Paris Editions Dervy, 2006). Although the Knoop, Jones and Hamer compilation prints transcriptions of the manuscripts, it does not have

much commentary, especially for the earliest material where it is most needed, whereas the Langlet compilation does. Langlet also notes the recurrence of various wordings from source to source, making his compilation more useful than the older English work-Langlet also presents the texts in the original as well as their French translation. Unfortunately, the projected second volume of Langlet's work has never appeared.

10. Béresniak, Daniel. *Le cabinet de réflexion : la démarche initiatique, technique de l'eveil* [The Chamber of Reflection: Initiatory Approach, Technique for Intellectual Awakening] (Paris, Editions Detrad aVs, 2004, DL 1995). Béresniak was a Past Grand Master of the Grande loge de France, an obedience American grand lodges do not recognize, although many did until the 1964-1966 period. This obedience practices the Scottish Rite exclusively in its blue lodges.

11. Béresniak, Daniel. *Rites et symboles de la Franc-maçonnerie, tome I: les loges bleues* (Paris, Editions Detrad aVs, 2005, DL 1995), p. 20-[42].

12. Mainguy, Irène. *La symbolique maçonnique du troisième millénaire* [Masonic symbolism for the Third Millennium] (Paris : Editions Dervy, c2001, reprinted 2005), p. [171]-187, *passim*. Mainguy is a librarian at the Grand Orient of France, an obedience that the Grand Lodge of Louisiana has not recognized since the 1870s, with the exception of part of World War I. The Grand Orient practices the French or Modern Rite (albeit in later revisions) in the vast majority of its blue lodges.

13. Pike, Albert. *The Porch and the Middle Chamber: the Book of the Lodge* (A.M. 5632, reprinted Kila, Mont., Kessinger Publishing, ca. 2008: 83)

14. My rather rough translation; there is no direct object for the "rectificando" although there should be; this fact has been noticed by a number of French writers and I have chosen "while purifying yourself" as reasonable.

15. In his *Trente-trois : histoire des degrés du Rite écossais ancien et accepté en France* (Les architectes de la connaissance. Groslay : Editions Ivoire-claire, 2004, p.154-157), Jean-Pierre Bayard (1920-2008) recounts his fantasies of terror at the appearance of this term ; since he had been an engineer he knew what "vitriol" was. In his *Le cabinet de réflexion : sa symbolique : la lumière des ténèbres* (Paris : Editions maçonniques de France, 2003 : 112-14), Bayard presents an exhaustive discussion of the meanings of V.I.T.R.I.O.L., its anagrams, and its extensions, such as V.I.T.R.I.O.L.U.M., and quotes at length from the article on VITRIOL in Antoine-Joseph Pernéty's *Dictionnaire mytho-hermétique* of 1758 (reprint: Milano: Archè, 1980), pp. 25-528, and the way in which Pernéty connects his definition with the pseudo-Hermetic *Tabula smaragdina* (Emerald Tablet), many of whose statements are to be found in the occultistic portions of various Scottish Rite degrees.

Masonic Communications

by Michael R. Poll, PM
Secretary, Louisiana Lodge of Research

WHEN I say something, the last thing I want is to be misunderstood. My goal is to always have the idea, thought or desire that is in my head given to the other clearly and correctly. If I would like someone to walk three houses down from where I live to a certain address and ask Mr. Jones if I can borrow a hammer, it would not serve me very well if I asked: "Go down there and bring me something from that guy." Where, what, who? If I want something in particular (and not just anything), then I need to be clear in how I communicate. On the other hand, if I wish to teach by the use of symbolism, then I may speak or write in a manner that will require the reader or listener to apply some thought to what I have offered. What is presented through symbolism could have more than one meaning and may not be obvious by design. How I communicate depends on my desired goal. Language is a tool that should be employed with some thought as to the desired effect in each particular instance.

So, what do we mean when we speak of "Masonic Communications"? Mind you, it is a very important question because as Masons we can't go around having "Masonic Communications" with just anyone. We have obligations which must be kept. We must understand what can be communicated to others and what is not allowed.

Of "communication," Albert Mackey tells us:

The meeting of a Lodge is so called. There is a peculiar significance in this term. To communicate, which, in the Old English form, was to common, originally meant to share in common with others. The great sacrament of the Christian Church, which denotes a participation in the mysteries of the religion and a fellowship in the church, is called a communion, which is fundamentally the same as a communication, for he who partakes of the communion is said to communicate. Hence the meetings of Masonic Lodges are called communications, to signify that it is not simply the ordinary meeting of a society for the transaction of business, but that such meeting is the fellowship of men engaged in a common pursuit, and governed by a common principle, and that there is therein a communication or participation of those feelings and sentiments that constitute a true brotherhood.[1]

Our Work teaches us that we are not to hold "Masonic Communications" with non-Masons or unrecognized/irregular/clandestine Masons. But, what exactly does that mean to us today? It is clear through our law that someone who is a Member of a lodge *not* in Fraternal Relations with our Grand Lodge cannot attend our meetings[2], but what are we allowed to say (communicate) to non-Masons and what is to be kept secret?

The Handbook of Masonic Law (Louisiana) tells us the following about the nature of a "secret":

"Secrecy applies to the modes of recognition, certain symbols, the ballot, obligations, signs, pass words, and the forms of initiation.[3]

There we have it. We are not to reveal any of the above to anyone unless we are certain that they are entitled to receive it. But, who are we talking about? Recognized/regular Masons? We know that someone is entitled to receive "the secrets" if we have sat in Lodge with them or if they have successfully passed a trial as taught to us in our ritual.

So, exactly who are those who we consider *unrecognized/irregular/clandestine*? These are often words that are used in Masonry interchangeably – even officially by Grand Lodges. Are they interchangeable? What exactly do they mean? While these words can mean the same thing, they each have their own specific meaning and can sometimes mean very different things. If we do not know when they can, or can't, be used interchangeably, we can run into confusion.

Fraternal Relations (recognition) is when two jurisdictions officially declare their satisfaction that each is regular. It is a treaty of friendship and acknowledgement that each is a legitimate Masonic body. It is a state that either exists or it does not. It is simple to determine. The Grand Lodge has a list of Masonic bodies which it "recognizes" and Members of which are allowed to visit our Lodges and with whom we may hold Masonic Communications - once we know them to be such. If a lodge is not on that list, they can not visit tiled lodges under the jurisdiction of the Grand Lodge of Louisiana. But, can we visit Lodges with unrecognized Masons? Is there any situation where we can legally hold Masonic Communications with members of unrecognized Lodges? The simple answer to the above questions is a surprising "yes" - at least according to our law book. It is sometimes called the "When in Rome Rule". From the *Louisiana Handbook on Masonic Law*:

> "Louisiana Masons, when traveling to other Grand Jurisdictions which are recognized as "Regular" by the Grand Lodge of the State of Louisiana, F.&A.M. and with which this Grand Lodge has established fraternal relations may, with the consent of the host Lodge or Grand Lodge, visit a tiled communication in any Lodge recognized as Regular by the Grand Lodge of Louisiana, F.&A.M. within that jurisdiction and, during the course thereof, exercise Masonic visitation with the Brethren who are recognized as Regular by that Grand Jurisdiction." [4]

This law was put in place due to the fact that of the 51 "mainstream" Grand Lodges in the United States, 42 of them (to date) have entered into Fraternal Relations with the Prince Hall Affiliate Grand Lodge in their state. They consider Prince Hall Affiliate Masons perfectly regular. Louisiana is one of the only 9 Grand Lodges in the United States which has not entered into Fraternal Relations with the Prince Hall Grand Lodge in their state. As such, if the "When in Rome Rule" did not exist in our Grand Lodge law, then visiting any of the Lodges in those 42 other Grand Lodges who *do* recognize Prince Hall in their state could be a problem. We could very easily be sitting in a Lodge and holding Masonic Communications with Masons not viewed as regular by our Grand Lodge (if we should equate *regular* with *recognized*) and that would be grounds for Masonic charges of violating our obligations. How could our Grand Master or other Grand Lodge Officers visit other jurisdictions? So, does this mean that we do or do not view Prince Hall as regular?

Regularity is a subjective state. It is not as clear to determine as we might think and certainly not as easy to determine as recognition. Grand Lodges, after examination, determine if a body is, or is not, regular - and, views on regularity can change. In an attempt to make the whole situation a bit easier to understand, Grand Lodges, years ago, seemed to become fond of linking regularity with recognition. If a body was recognized, then it was viewed as regular. If it was not recognized, then it was said to be irregular or clandestine. Most of the time, this works fine. But, every now and then, we are bitten if we never allow for the exception. The "When in Rome Rule" is a clear example of how we can't always clearly look to recognition to determine regularity. Logic dictates that if the Grand Lodge of Louisiana considers Prince Hall Affiliate Masonry to be irregular then our own law presents a situation where we are allowed to hold Masonic Communications with those who we consider to be irregular. Is that what we are saying? That would seem to be a violation of our Obligations.

Louisiana has a written record of declaring at least one Grand Lodge regular with whom Fraternal Relations had not yet been established. If we look at the Grand Lodge of Louisiana Proceedings from 1955, we can find that the National Grand Lodge in France was deemed by Louisiana to be regular, yet Fraternal Relations were not then offered or existing.[5] Yep, they were deemed *regular*, but they were not *recognized*. Lack of recognition has *not* always officially meant irregularity.

To be irregular means that there is something wrong with the body. It could be a problem with the work, or the lineage (how they were created) or any other matter that would present a problem to anyone seeking to determine if they are a valid Masonic body. It could be a minor, fixable problem or it could be a problem of such severity that the body would be deemed hopeless and not able to be saved.

And what of the word "clandestine"? Yes, it is very often used with or in place of "irregular." But, it has a much more specific meaning. When the Soviet Union broke apart, an interesting thing happened. All of a sudden hands started popping up. The hands belonged to Masonic lodges that had existed in the Soviet Union underground. Freemasonry was outlawed and had these lodges been discovered, the members would have been in serious trouble. But, they kept Freemasonry alive by working in secret. These are true clandestine lodges - hidden lodges. Yes, in the most technical sense, they were irregular as they operated under no Grand Lodge authority. But as soon as they were discovered, the European Grand Lodges lined up to take them in. They realized that the "problem" was an easy fix and these Masons were worthy of great respect and not condemnation.

At the writing of this paper, Fraternal Relations between the Most Worshipful Grand Lodge of the State of Louisiana, F&AM and the Most Worshipful Prince Hall Grand Lodge of Louisiana, F&AM do not exist. The law of the Grand Lodge of Louisiana is clear that members of Lodges under any Prince Hall Grand Lodge can not sit in one of our tiled lodges. Yet, the law is also clear that situations can arise where it is permitted for members of lodges under the Grand Lodge of Louisiana to sit in tiled lodges with Masons under the jurisdiction of a Prince Hall Grand Lodge. When we sit in a tiled lodge, "Masonic Communications" (by however they are defined) are taking place. At the opening of this paper, I pointed out the problems that can arise when we are not perfectly clear in the expressions of our desires. It would seem that a contradiction exists in our law and obligations. On one hand, we are told that under certain situations we are allowed to hold Masonic Communications with unrecognized Masons, yet in another aspect of our law, we are told that we are not allowed to hold Masonic Communications with an unrecognized Mason. Neither directive references the other nor provides an explanation to the apparent contradiction.

Freemasonry in the United States is in a time of remarkable evolution. Communications in general have dramatically changed with the advent of cell phones, the internet and a host of new electronic gadgets. With the recognition of Prince Hall Masonry by the vast majority of U.S. Grand Lodges, our understanding of Masonic Communications has, by practicality, undergone a reevaluation and resulted in an evolution of practice. It is clearly not a perfect solution and is open to numerous charges of contradictory and illogical practices, but it is a work in progress. It is a step.

Should the Grand Lodge of Louisiana and the Prince Hall Grand Lodge of Louisiana clear up this apparent contradiction and officially enter into Fraternal Relations? This writer has his personal opinion, but it is really a question for the two Grand Lodges. What is it that they both desire?

Fraternal Recognition is a two way street. *Both* sides must desire it and work to its end. We would be kidding ourselves if we believed that racism played no part at all in keeping both sides apart. Those who have bigotry in their hearts (on either side) are kidding themselves if they believe that their view of Freemasonry plays any part in its future.

So, what do we want? It is a question we must all answer sooner or later.

NOTES

1. Albert G. Mackey, *An Encyclopedia of Freemasonry and its Kindred Sciences Vol. I* (New York: The Masonic History Company, 1925) 170.
2. "One who is a member of a Lodge under the jurisdiction of a Grand Lodge not in fraternal relations with the Grand Lodge of Louisiana, shall not be permitted to visit any of the Lodge of Louisiana." *The Handbook of Masonic Law* (Alexandria, LA: The Grand Lodge of the State of Louisiana, F&AM 2012) 110.
3. Ibid., iv b
4. Ibid 110.
5. "We do not question the regularity of the French National Grand Lodge - their recognition by 41 of the Grand Lodges of the United States attests to that. We are not ready, however, to suggest that the Grand Lodge of Louisiana sever the cordial relationship of long standing with the Grand Lodge of France. In the hope that union of the two French Grand Lodges may yet be consummated, WE RECOMMEND NO CHANGE BE MADE IN OUR FRATERNAL RELATIONSHIP WITH THE GRAND LODGE OF FRANCE.: (Caps in original text) *Proceedings of the Grand Lodge of the State of Louisiana, 1955.* (New Orleans, LA: The Grand Lodge of the State of Louisiana, F&AM, 1955) 180.

Regius Manuscript

by H. L. Haywood

IN 1757 King George II presented to the British Museum a collection of some 12,000 volumes, the nucleus of which had been laid by King Henry VII and which came to be known as the Royal Library. Among these books was a rarely beautiful manuscript written by hand on 64 pages of vellum, about four by five inches in size, which a cataloger, David Casley, entered as No. 17 A-1 under the title, "A Poem of Moral Duties: here entitled Constitutiones Artis Gemetrie Secundem." It was not until Mr. J.O. Halliwell, F.R.S. (afterwards Halliwell-Phillipps), a non-Mason, chanced to make the discovery that the manuscript was known to be a masonic document. Mr. Phillipps read a paper on the manuscript before the Society of Antiquaries in 1839, and in the following year published a volume entitled Early History of Freemasonry in England (enlarged and revised in 1844), in which he incorporated a transcript of the document along with a few pages in facsimile. This important work will be found incorporated in the familiar Universal Masonic Library, the rusty sheepskin bindings of which strike the eyes on almost every masonic book shelf. This manuscript was known as "The Halliwell", or as "The Halliwell-Phillipps" until some fifty years atfterwards Gould rechristened it, in honour of the Royal Library in which it is found, the "Regius", and since then this has become the more familiar cognomen.

David Casley, a learned specialist in old manuscripts, dated the "Regius" as of the fourteenth century. E.A. Bond, another expert, dated it as of the middle of the fifteenth century. Dr. Kloss, the German specialist, placed it between 1427 and 1445. But the majority have agreed on 1390 as the most probable date. "It is impossible to arrive at absolute certainty on this point," says Hughan, whose Old Charges should be consulted, "save that it is not likely to be older than 1390, but may be some twenty years or so later." Dr. W. Begemann made a study of the document that has never been equalled for thoroughness, and arrived at a conclusion that may be given in his own words: it was written "towards the end of the 14th or at least quite at the beginning of the 15th century (not in Gloucester itself, as being too southerly, but) in the north of Gloucestershire or in the neighbouring north of Herefordshire, or even possibly in the south of Worcestershire." (A.Q.C. VII, page 35.)

In 1889 an exact facsimile of this famous manuscript was published in Volume I of the Antigrapha produced by the Quatuor Coronati Lodge of Research, and was edited by the then secretary of that lodge, George William Speth, himself a brilliant authority, who supplied a glossary that is indispensable to the amateur student. Along with it was published a commentary by R. F. Gould, one of the greatest of all his masonic papers, though it is exasperating in its rambling arrangement and general lack of conclusiveness.

The Regius Manuscript is the only one of all the versions to be written in meter, and may have been composed by a priest, if one may judge by certain internal evidences, though the point is disputed. There are some 800 lines in the poem, the strictly masonic portion coming to an end at line 576, after which begins what Hughan calls a "sermonette" on moral duties, in which there is quite a Roman Catholic vein with references to "the sins seven", "the sweet lady" (referring to the Virgin) and to holy water. There is no such specific Mariolatry in any other version of the Old Charges, though the great majority of them express loyalty to "Holy Church" and all of them, until Anderson's familiar version, are specifically Christian, so far as religion is concerned.

The author furnishes a list of fifteen "points" and fifteen "articles", all of which are quite specific instructions concerning the behaviour of a Craftsman: this portion is believed by many to have been the charges to an initiate as used in the author's period, and is therefore deemed the most important feature of the book as furnishing us a picture of the regulations of the Craft at that remote date. The Craft is described as having come into existence as an organized fraternity in "King Adelstoune's day", but in this the author contradicts himself, because he refers to things "written in old books" (I modernize spelling of quotations) and takes for granted a certain antiquity for the Masonry, which, as in all the Old Charges, is made synonymous with Geometry, a thing very different in those days from the abstract science over which we laboured during our school days.

The Regius Poem is evidently a book about Masonry, rather than a document of Masonry, and may very well have been written by a non-mason, though there is no way in which we can verify such theories, especially seeing that we know nothing about the document save what it has to tell us about itself, which is little.

In his Commentary on the Regius MS, R. F. Gould produced a paragraph that has ever since served as the pivot of a great debate. It reads as follows and refers to the "sermonette" portion which deals with "moral duties": "These rules of decorum read very curiously in the present age, but their inapplicability to the circumstances of the working masons of the fourteen or fifteenth century will be at once apparent. They were intended for the gentlemen of those days, and the instruction for behaviour in the presence of a lord-at table and in the society of ladies-would have all been equally out of place in a code of manners drawn up for the use of a Guild or Craft of Artisans."

The point of this is that there must have been present among the Craftsmen of that time a number of men not engaged at all in labour, and therefore were, as we would now describe them, "speculatives." This would be of immense importance if Gould had made good his point, but that he was not able to do. The greatest minds of the period in question were devoted to architecture, and there is no reason not to believe that among the Craftsmen were members of good families.

Also the Craft was in contact with the clergy all the while, and therefore many of its members may well have stood in need of rules for preserving proper decorum in great houses and among the members of the upper classes. From Woodford until the present time the great majority of masonic scholars have believed the Old Charges to have been used by a strictly operative craft and it is evident that they will continue to do so until more conclusive evidence to the contrary is forthcoming than Gould's surmise.

Regius Manuscript 1390
A POEM OF MORAL DUTIES
(in modern English)

Here begin the constitutions of the art
of Geometry according to Euclid.

Whoever will both well read and look
He may find written in old book
Of great lords and also ladies,

That had many children together, certainly;
And had no income to keep them with,
Neither in town nor field nor enclosed wood;
A council together they could them take,
To ordain for these children's sake,
How they might best lead their life
Without great disease, care and strife;
And most for the multitude that was coming
Of their children after great clerks,
To teach them then good works;

And pray we them, for our Lord's sake.
To our children some work to make,
That they might get their living thereby,
Both well and honestly full securely.
In that time, through good geometry,
This honest craft of good masonry
Was ordained and made in this manner,
Counterfeited of these clerks together;
At these lord's prayers they counter-
feited geometry,
And gave it the name of masonry,
For the most honest craft of all.
These lords' children thereto did fall,
To learn of him the craft of geometry,
The which he made full curiously;

Through fathers' prayers and mothers' also,
This honest craft he put them to.
He learned best, and was of honesty,
And passed his fellows in curiosity,
If in that craft he did him pass,
He should have more worship than the less,
This great clerk's name was Euclid,
His name it spread full wonder wide.
Yet this great clerk ordained he
To him that was higher in this degree,
That he should teach the simplest of wit
In that honest craft to be perfect;
And so each one shall teach the other,

And love together as sister and brother.

Futhermore yet that ordained he,
Master called so should he be;
So that he were most worshipped,
Then should he be so called;
But masons should never one another call,
Within the craft amongst them all,
Neither subject nor servant, my dear brother,
Though he be not so perfect as is another;
Each shall call other fellows by friendship,
Because they come of ladies' birth.
On this manner, through good wit of geometry,
Began first the craft of masonry;
The clerk Euclid on this wise it found,
This craft of geometry in Egypt land.

In Egypt he taught it full wide,
In divers lands on every side;
Many years afterwards, I understand,
Ere that the craft came into this land.
This craft came into England, as I you say,
In time of good King Athelstane's day;
He made then both hall and even bower,
And high temples of great honour,
To disport him in both day and night,
And to worship his God with all his might.
This good lord loved this craft full well,
And purposed to strengthen it every part,
For divers faults that in the craft he found;
He sent about into the land

After all the masons of the craft,
To come to him full even straight,
For to amend these defaults all
By good counsel, if it might fall.
An assembly then could let make
Of divers lords in their state,
Dukes, earls, and barons also,
Knights, squires and many more,

And the great burgesses of that city,
They were there all in their degree;
There were there each one always,
To ordain for these masons' estate,
There they sought by their wit,
How they might govern it;

Fifteen articles they there sought,
And fifteen points there they wrought,

Here begins the first article.

The first article of this geometry;-
The master mason must be full securely
Both steadfast, trusty and true,
It shall him never then rue;
And pay thy fellows after the cost,
As victuals goeth then, well thou knowest;
And pay them truly, upon thy faith,
What they may deserve;
And to their hire take no more,
But what that they may serve for;
And spare neither for love nor dread,

Of neither parties to take no bribe;
Of lord nor fellow, whoever he be,
Of them thou take no manner of fee;
And as a judge stand upright,
And then thou dost to both good right;
And truly do this wheresoever thou goest,
Thy worship, thy profit, it shall be most.

Second article.

The second article of good masonry,
As you must it here hear specially,
That every master, that is a mason,
Must be at the general congregation,
So that he it reasonably be told
Where that the assembly shall be held;

And to that assembly he must needs go,
Unless he have a reasonable excuse,
Or unless he be disobedient to that craft
Or with falsehood is overtaken,
Or else sickness hath him so strong,
That he may not come them among;
That is an excuse good and able,
To that assembly without fable.

Third article.

The third article forsooth it is,
That the master takes to no 'prentice,
Unless he have good assurance to dwell
Seven years with him, as I you tell,
His craft to learn, that is profitable;

Within less he may no be able
To lords' profit, nor to his own
As you may know by good reason.

Fourth article.

The fourth article this must be,
That the master him well besee,
That he no bondman 'prentice make,
Nor for no covetousness do him take;
For the lord that he is bound to,
May fetch the 'prentice wheresoever he go.
If in the lodge he were taken,
Much disease it might there make,
And such case it might befall,
That it might grieve some or all.

For all the masons that be there
Will stand together all together.
If such one in that craft should dwell,
Of divers disease you might tell;
For more ease then, and of honesty,

Take a 'prentice of higher degree.
By old time written I find
That the 'prentice should be of gentle kind;
And so sometime, great lords' blood
Took this geometry that is full good.

Fifth article.

The fifth article is very good,
So that the 'prentice be of lawful blood;
The master shall not, for no advantage,

Make no 'prentice that is deformed;
It is mean, as you may hear
That he have all his limbs whole all together;
To the craft it were great shame,
To make a halt man and a lame,
For an imperfect man of such blood
Should do the craft but little good.
Thus you may know every one,
The craft would have a mighty man;
A maimed man he hath no might,
You must it know long ere night.

Sixth article.

The sixth article you must not miss

That the master do the lord no prejudice,
To take the lord for his 'prentice,
As much as his fellows do, in all wise.
For in that craft they be full perfect,
So is not he, you must see it.
Also it were against good reason,
To take his hire as his fellows do.

This same article in this case,
Judgeth his prentice to take less
Than his fellows, that be full perfect.
In divers matters, know require it,

The master may his 'prentice so inform,
That his hire may increase full soon,
And ere his term come to an end,
His hire may full well amend.

Seventh article.

The seventh article that is now here,
Full well will tell you all together,
That no master for favour nor dread,
Shall no thief neither clothe nor feed.
Thieves he shall harbour never one,
Nor him that hath killed a man,
Nor the same that hath a feeble name,
Lest it would turn the craft to shame.

Eighth article.

The eighth article sheweth you so,
That the master may it well do.
If that he have any man of craft,
And he be not so perfect as he ought,
He may him change soon anon,
And take for him a more perfect man.
Such a man through recklessness,
Might do the craft scant worship.

Ninth article.

The ninth article sheweth full well,
That the master be both wise and strong;
That he no work undertake,
Unless he can both it end and make;
And that it be to the lords' profit also,
And to his craft, wheresoever he go;
And that the ground be well taken,
That it neither flaw nor crack.

Tenth article.

The tenth article is for to know,
Among the craft, to high and low,
There shall no master supplant another,
But be together as sister and brother,
In this curious craft, all and some,
That belongeth to a master mason.
Nor shall he supplant no other man,
That hath taken a work him upon,
In pain thereof that is so strong,

That weigheth no less than ten pounds,
but if that he be guilty found,
That took first the work on hand;
For no man in masonry
Shall not supplant other securely,
But if that it be so wrought,
That in turn the work to nought;
Then may a mason that work crave,
To the lords' profit for it to save
In such a case if it do fall,
There shall no mason meddle withal.
Forsooth he that beginneth the ground,
If he be a mason good and sound,
He hath it securely in his mind

To bring the work to full good end.

Eleventh article.

The eleventh article I tell thee,
That he is both fair and free;
For he teacheth, by his might,
That no mason should work by night,
But if be in practising of wit,
If that I could amend it.

Twelfth article.

The twelfth article is of high honesty
To every mason wheresoever he be,
He shall not his fellows' work deprave,
If that he will his honesty save;
With honest words he it commend,

By the wit God did thee send;
But it amend by all that thou may,
Between you both without doubt.

Thirteenth article.

The thirteenth article, so God me save,
Is if that the master a 'prentice have,
Entirely then that he him tell,
That he the craft ably may know,
Wheresoever he go under the sun.

Fourteenth article.

The fourteenth article by good reason,
Sheweth the master how he shall do;
He shall no 'prentice to him take,
Unless diver cares he have to make,
That he may within his term,
Of him divers points may learn.

Fifteenth article.

The fifteenth article maketh an end,
For to the master he is a friend;
To teach him so, that for no man,
No false maintenance he take him upon,
Nor maintain his fellows in their sin,
For no good that he might win;
Nor no false oath suffer him to make,
For dread of their souls' sake,
Lest it would turn the craft to shame,

And himself to very much blame.

Plural constitutions.

At this assembly were points ordained more,
Of great lords and masters also.
That who will know this craft and come to estate,
He must love well God and holy church always,
And his master also that he is with,
Whersoever he go in field or enclosed wood,
And thy fellows thou love also,
For that thy craft will that thou do.

Second Point.

The second point as I you say,
That the mason work upon the work day,
As truly as he can or may,

To deserve his hire for the holy-day,
And truly to labour on his deed,
Well deserve to have his reward.

Third point.

The third point must be severely,
With the 'prentice know it well,
His master's counsel he keep and close,
And his fellows by his good purpose;
The privities of the chamber tell he no man,
Nor in the lodge whatsoever they do;
Whatsoever thou hearest or seest them do,
Tell it no man wheresoever you go;
The counsel of hall, and even of bower,

Keep it well to great honour,
Lest it would turn thyself to blame,
And bring the craft into great shame.

Fourth point.

The fourth point teacheth us also,
That no man to his craft be false;
Error he shall maintain none
Against the craft, but let it go;
Nor no prejudice he shall no do
To his master, nor his fellow also;
And though the 'prentice be under awe,
Yet he would have the same law.

Fifth point.

The fifth point is without doubt,
That when the mason taketh his pay
Of the master, ordained to him,
Full meekly taken so must it be;
Yet must the master by good reason,
Warn him lawfully before noon,
If he will not occupy him no more,
As he hath done there before;
Against this order he may no strive,
If he think well for to thrive.

Sixth point.

The sixth point is full given to know,
Both to high and even low,

For such case it might befall;
Among the masons some or all,
Through envy or deadly hate,
Oft ariseth full great debate.
Then ought the mason if that he may,
Put them both under a day;
But loveday yet shall they make none,
Till that the work-day you must well take
Leisure enough loveday to make,
Hinder their work for such a fray;
To such end then that you them draw.

That they stand well in God's law.

Seventh point.

The seventh point he may well mean,
Of well long life that God us lend,
As it descrieth well openly,
Thou shalt not by thy master's wife lie,
Nor by thy fellows', in no manner wise,
Lest the craft would thee despise;
Nor by thy fellows' concubine,
No more thou wouldst he did by thine.
The pain thereof let it be sure,
That he be 'prentice full seven year,
If he forfeit in any of them
So chastised then must he be;
Full much care might there begin,
For such a foul deadly sin.

Eighth point.

The eighth point, he may be sure,
If thou hast taken any cure,
Under thy master thou be true,
For that point thous shalt never rue;
A true mediator thou must needs be
To thy master, and thy fellows free;
Do truly all that thou might,
To both parties, and that is good right.

Ninth point.

The ninth point we shall him call,
That he be steward of our hall,
If that you be in chamber together,
Each one serve other with mild cheer;
Gentle fellows, you must it know,
For to be stewards all in turn,
Week after week without doubt,
Stewards to be so all in turn about,

Amiably to serve each one other,
As though they were sister and brother;
There shall never one another cost
Free himself to no advantage,
But every man shall be equally free
In that cost, so must it be;
Look that thou pay well every man always,
That thou hast bought any victuals eaten,
That no craving be made to thee,
Nor to thy fellows in no degree,
To man or to woman, whoever he be,
Pay them well and truly, for that will we;
Therof on thy fellow true record thou take,
For that good pay as thou dost make,
Lest it would thy fellow shame,
And bring thyself into great blame.
Yet good accounts he must make
Of such goods as he hath taken,

Of thy fellows' goods that thou hast spent,
Where and how and to what end;
Such accounts thou must come to,
When thy fellows wish that thou do.

Tenth point.

The tenth point presenteth well good life,
To live without care and strife;
For if the mason live amiss,
And in his work be false I know,

And through such a false excuse
May slander his fellows without reason,
Through false slander of such fame

May make the craft acquire blame.
If he do the craft such villainy,
Do him no favour then securely,
Nor maintain not him in wicked life,
Lest it would turn to care and strife;

But yet him you shall not delay,
Unless that you shall him constrain,
For to appear wheresoever you will,
Where that you will, loud, or still;
To the next assembly you him call,
To appear before his fellows all,
And unless he will before them appear,

The craft he must need forswear;
He shall then be punished after the law
That was founded by old day.

Eleventh point.

The eleventh point is of good discretion,
As you must know by good reason;
A mason, if he this craft well know,
That seeth his fellow hew on a stone,
And is in point to spoil that stone,
Amend it soon if that thou can,
And teach him then it to amend,
That the lords' work be not spoiled,
And teach him easily it to amend,

With fair words, that God thee hath lent;
For his sake that sit above,
With sweet words nourish his love.

Twelfth point.

The twelfth point is of great royalty,
There as the assembly held shall be,
There shall be masters and fellows also,
And other great lords many more;
There shall be the sheriff of that country,
And also the mayor of that city,
Knights and squires there shall be,

And also aldermen, as you shall see;
Such ordinance as thy make there,

They shall maintain it all together
Against that man, whatsoever he be,
That belongeth to the craft both fair and
free.
If he any strife against them make,
Into their custody he shall be taken.

Thirteenth point.

The thirteenth point is to us full lief,
He shall swear never to be no thief,
Nor succour him in his false craft,
For no good that he hath bereft,
And thou must it know or sin,
Neither for his good, nor for his kin.

Fourteenth point.

The fourteenth point is full good law
To him that would be under awe;
A good true oath he must there swear
To his master and his fellows that be there;
He must be steadfast be and true also
To all this ordinance, wheresoever he go,
And to his liege lord the king,
To be true to him over all thing.
And all these points here before
To them thou must need be sworn,
And all shall swear the same oath
Of the masons, be they lief be they loath.
To all these points here before,

That hath been ordained by full good lore.
And they shall enquire every man
Of his party, as well as he can,
If any man may be found guilty
In any of these points specially;
And who he be, let him be sought,
And to the assembly let him be brought.

Fifteen point.

The fifteenth point is full good lore,
For them that shall be there sworn,
Such ordinance at the assembly was laid
Of great lords and masters before said;
For the same that be disobedient, I know,

Against the ordinance that there is,
Of these articles that were moved there,
Of great lords and masons all together,
And if they be proved openly
Before that assembly, by and by,
And for their guilt's no amends will make,
Then must they need the craft forsake;
And no masons craft they shall refuse,
And swear it never more to use.
But if that they will amends make,
Again to the craft they shall never take;
And if that they will no do so,
The sheriff shall come them soon to,

And put their bodies in deep prison,
For the trespass that they have done,
And take their goods and their cattle
Into the king's hand, every part,
And let them dwell there full still,
Till it be our liege king's will.

Another ordinance of the art of geometry.

They ordained there an assembly to be hold,
Every year, wheresoever they would,
To amend the defaults, if any were found
Among the craft within the land;
Each year or third year it should be held,

In every place weresoever they would;
Time and place must be ordained also,
In what place they should assemble to,

All the men of craft there they must be,
And other great lords, as you must see,
To mend the faults the he there spoken,
If that any of them be then broken.
There they shall be all sworn,
That belongeth to this craft's lore,
To keep their statutes every one
That were ordained by King Althelstane;
These statutes that I have here found

I ordain they be held through my land,
For the worship of my royalty,
That I have by my dignity.
Also at every assembly that you hold,
That you come to your liege king bold,
Beseeching him of his grace,
To stand with you in every place,
To confirm the statutes of King Athelstane,
That he ordained to this craft by good reason.

The art of the four crowned ones.

Pray we now to God almighty,
And to his mother Mary bright,

That we may keep these articles here,
And these points well all together,
As did these holy martyrs four,
That in this craft were of great honour;
They were as good masons as on earth shall go,
Gravers and image-makers they were also.
For they were workmen of the best,
The emperor had to them great liking;
He willed of them an image to make
That might be worshipped for his sake;
Such monuments he had in his day,
To turn the people from Christ's law.

But they were steadfast in Christ's law,

And to their craft without doubt;
They loved well God and all his lore,
And were in his service ever more.
True men they were in that day,
And lived well in God's law;
They thought no monuments for to make,
For no good that they might take,
To believe on that monument for their God,
They would not do so, though he was furious;
For they would not forsake their true faith,

And believe on his false law,
The emperor let take them soon anon,
And put them in a deep prison;
The more sorely he punished them in that place,
The more joy was to them of Christ's grace,
Then when he saw no other one,
To death he let them then go;
By the book he might it show
In legend of holy ones,
The names of the four-crowned ones.

Their feast will be without doubt,
After Hallow-e'en eighth day.
You may hear as I do read,
That many years after, for great dread
That Noah's flood was all run,
The tower of Babylon was begun,
As plain work of lime and stone,
As any man should look upon;
So long and broad it was begun,
Seven miles the height shadoweth the sun.
King Nebuchadnezzar let it make
To great strength for man's sake,
Though such a flood again should come,
Over the work it should not take;
For they had so high pride, with strong
boast
All that work therefore was lost;

An angel smote them so with divers speech,
That never one knew what the other should
tell.
Many years after, the good clerk Euclid
Taught the craft of geometry full wonder wide,
So he did that other time also,
Of divers crafts many more.
Through high grace of Christ in heaven,
He commenced in the sciences seven;

Grammar is the first science I know,
Dialect the second, so I have I bliss,
Rhetoric the third without doubt,
Music is the fourth, as I you say,

Astronomy is the fifth, by my snout,
Arithmetic the sixth, without doubt,
Geometry the seventh maketh an end,
For he is both meek and courteous,
Grammar forsooth is the root,
Whoever will learn on the book;
But art passeth in his degree,
As the fruit doth the root of the tree;

Rhetoric measureth with ornate speech among,
And music it is a sweet song;
Astronomy numbereth, my dear brother,
Arithmetic sheweth one thing that is another,
Geometry the seventh science it is,
That can separate falsehood from truth, I know
These be the sciences seven,
Who useth them well he may have heaven.
Now dear children by your wit
Pride and covetousness that you leave it,
And taketh heed to good discretion,
And to good nurture, wheresoever you come.
Now I pray you take good heed,

For this you must know needs,

But much more you must know,
Than you find here written.
If thee fail therto wit,
Pray to God to send thee it;
For Christ himself, he teacheth us
That holy church is God's house,
That is made for nothing else
But for to pray in, as the book tells us;
There the people shall gather in,
To pray and weep for their sin.
Look thou come not to church late,
For to speak harlotry by the gate;

Then to church when thou dost fare,
Have in thy mind ever more
To worship thy lord God both day and night,
With all thy wits and even thy might.
To the church door when thou dost come
Of that holy water there some thou take,
For every drop thou feelest there
Quencheth a venial sin, be thou sure.
But first thou must do down thy hood,
For his love that died on the rood.
Into the church when thou dost go,
Pull up thy heart to Christ, anon;

Upon the rood thou look up then,
And kneel down fair upon thy knees,
Then pray to him so here to work,
After the law of holy church,

For to keep the commandments ten,
That God gave to all men;
And pray to him with mild voice
To keep thee from the sins seven,
That thou here may, in this life,
Keep thee well from care and strife;
Furthermore he grant thee grace,
In heaven's bliss to have a place.

In holy church leave trifling words
Of lewd speech and foul jests,
And put away all vanity,
And say thy pater noster and thine ave;
Look also that thou make no noise,
But always to be in thy prayer;
If thou wilt not thyself pray,
Hinder no other man by no way.
In that place neither sit nor stand,
But kneel fair down on the ground,
And when the Gospel me read shall,

Fairly thou stand up from the wall,
And bless the fare if that thou can,
When gloria tibi is begun;
And when the gospel is done,
Again thou might kneel down,
On both knees down thou fall,
For his love that bought us all;
And when thou hearest the bell ring
To that holy sacrament,
Kneel you must both young and old,
And both your hands fair uphold,
And say then in this manner,

Fair and soft without noise;
"Jesu Lord welcome thou be,
In form of bread as I thee see,
Now Jesu for thine holy name,
Shield me from sin and shame;
Shrift and Eucharist thou grand me both,
Ere that I shall hence go,
And very contrition for my sin,
That I never, Lord, die therein;
And as thou were of maid born,
Suffer me never to be lost;
But when I shall hence wend,

Grant me the bliss without end;
Amen! Amen! so mote it be!
Now sweet lady pray for me."
Thus thou might say, or some other thing,
When thou kneelest at the sacrament.
For covetousness after good, spare thou not
To worship him that all hath wrought;

For glad may a man that day be,
That once in the day may him see;
It is so much worth, without doubt,
The virtue thereof no man tell may;
But so much good doth that sight,

That Saint Austin telleth full right,
That day thou seest God's body,
Thou shalt have these full securely:-
Meet and drink at thy need,
None that day shalt thou lack;
Idle oaths and words both,
God forgiveth thee also;
Sudden death that same day
Thee dare not dread by no way;
Also that day, I thee plight,
Thou shalt not lose thy eye sight;
And each foot that thou goest then,

That holy sight for to see,
They shall be told to stand instead,
When thou hast thereto great need;
That messenger the angel Gabriel,
Will keep them to thee full well.
From this matter now I may pass,
To tell more benefits of the mass:
To church come yet, if thou may,
And hear the mass each day;
If thou may not come to church,
Where that ever thou dost work,
When thou hearest the mass toll,

Pray to God with heart still,
To give thy part of that service,
That in church there done is.
Furthermore yet, I will you preach
To your fellows, it for to teach,
When thou comest before a lord,
In hall, in bower, or at the board,
Hood or cap that thou off do,
Ere thou come him entirely to;
Twice or thrice, without doubt,
To that lord thou must bow;
With thy right knee let it be done,

Thine own worship thou save so.
Hold off thy cap and hood also,
Till thou have leave it on to put.
All the time thou speakest with him,
Fair and amiably hold up thy chin;
So after the nurture of the book,
In his face kindly thou look.
Foot and hand thou keep full still,
For clawing and tripping, is skill;
From spitting and sniffling keep thee also,
By private expulsion let it go,
And if that thou be wise and discrete,

Thou has great need to govern thee well.
Into the hall when thou dost wend,
Amongst the gentles, good and courteous,
Presume not too high for nothing,
For thine high blood, nor thy cunning,
Neither to sit nor to lean,
That is nurture good and clean.
Let not thy countenance therefor abate,
Forsooth good nurture will save thy state.
Father and mother, whatsoever they be,
Well is the child that well may thee,
In hall, in chamber, where thou dost go;

Good manners make a man.
To the next degree look wisely,
To do them reverence by and by;
Do them yet no reverence all in turn,
Unless that thou do them know.
To the meat when thou art set,
Fair and honestly thou eat it;
First look that thine hands be clean,
And that thy knife be sharp and keen,
And cut thy bread all at thy meat,
Right as it may be there eaten,
If thou sit by a worthier man,

Then thy self thou art one,
Suffer him first to touch the meat,
Ere thyself to it reach.
To the fairest morsel thou might not strike,
Though that thou do it well like;
Keep thine hands fair and well,
From foul smudging of thy towel;
Thereon thou shalt not thy nose blow,
Nor at the meat thy tooth thou pick;
Too deep in cup thou might not sink,
Though thou have good will to drink,
Lest thine eyes would water thereby-

Then were it no courtesy.
Look in thy mouth there be no meat,
When thou begins to drink or speak.
When thou seest any man drinking,
That taketh heed to thy speech,
Soon anaon thou cease thy tale,
Whether he drink wine or ale,
Look also thou scorn no man,
In what degree thou seest him gone;
Nor thou shalt no man deprave,
If thou wilt thy worship save;
For such word might there outburst.

That might make thee sit in evil rest.
Close thy hand in thy fist,
And keep thee well from "had I known."
Hold thy tongue and spend thy sight;
Laugh thou not with no great cry,
Nor make no lewd sport and ribaldry.
Play thou not but with thy peers,
Nor tell thou not all that thou hears;
Discover thou not thine own deed,
For no mirth, nor for no reward;
With fair speech thou might have thy will,
With it thou might thy self spoil.

When thou meetest a worthy man,
Cap and hood thou hold not on;
In church, in market, or in the gate,
Do him reverance after his state.
If thou goest with a worthier man
Then thyself thou art one,
Let thy foremost shoulder follow his back,
For that is nurture without lack;

When he doth speak, hold thee still,
When he hath done, say for thy will,
In thy speech that thou be discreet,
And what thou sayest consider thee well;
But deprive thou not him his tale,
Neither at the wine nor at the ale.
Christ then of his high grace,
Save you both wit and space,
Well this book to know and read,
Heaven to have for your reward.
Amen! Amen! so mote it be!
So say we all for charity.

The Mystery of Freemasonry

by Clayton J. Borne, III, 33°, PGM
Worshipful Master, Louisiana Lodge of Research

FROM the earliest of times Man has challenged the reason for his existence. He faced his humanness desperately attempting to understand himself and his place in the universe. Man was perplexed by having to view his existence confronted by an ever present battle between good and evil. Man learned through experience to distinguish between ignorance and knowledge.

From the earliest of times historians have deemed these academic challenges, the Mysteries. As Freemasons we see these questions brought to light in the allegories of our Ritual. Our purpose as Masons should be to boldly challenge these philosophical questions in order to truly understand ourselves and in so doing master the "Mystery of Freemasonry."

In its' most basic form man's journey to enlightenment has been a search for meaning, insight, personal awareness, and spiritual development. Simply put it is the quest for and the journey to personal happiness.

For thousands of years historians have recorded dynamic civilizations wherein the people were dedicated to understanding these philosophical principles. Interestingly to us as Masons many of these advanced societies were integrated with artesian or operative components. These cultures with their philosophical and operative influences developed the very principles used by our spiritual brotherhood today.

Who were these dynamic people that influenced the development of our Fraternal Brotherhood? They were the Hamitic Egyptians (4000 BC) that migrated to all parts of the Mediterranean to be known as the Etruscans in Italy, the Pelasgoi in Greece, and the Hittities in Asia all of whom were referred to by historians as the "Temple Builders". The Zoroastiean Societies (3000 BC) in Persia, the Rosicrucian Societies in Egypt (1500 BC), the Druids (1000 BC)in the British Isles and the Essene Societies (200 BC)are well known classic evidences of spiritually motivated, disciplined societies, all having an artesian component.

It is my sincere belief that as a philosophy of life, the challenge and discipline of understanding human existence began at that moment in time when the Grand Architect of the Universe gave or developed in early man that unique quality which would separate him from the rest of his creation, namely a rational conscience. Man was then able to then exercise the spiritual quality of desiring and being able to choose good over evil, and in so doing being able to render obedience to the will of his Creator. This principle of consciousness awakening was then, just as today, at the core of the Masonic discipline and the core principle of Free Masonry.

It is clear therefore that the craft's teaching and philosophy preceded its formal organization by thousands of years. Reaching that point in history which we refer to as the "Operative Period" and the emergence of trade guilds the alliance of virtue and common ideals had finally developed a distinct and most dynamic identity.

This quest for virtue by modern man is only possible through an insistence and reliance on the principle of truth as a defined spiritual objective. It is only in this search that man can have continued spiritual and intellectual growth.

Does the Philosophy of Freemasonry accomplish these objectives? In other words is Freemasonry addressing the most basic questions of human existence for our spiritual Brotherhood and collectively the brotherhood of man? To properly address this question we must examine our fraternity from the standpoint of what it is not. Masonic historians see our fraternity as having developed differently in different parts of the world, and I believe it certainly has. Philosophical, Sociological, and Philanthropically characteristics have in fact developed in response to the progress, needs and demands of different societies.

It has been written however that in a most basic or fundamental sense Freemasonry is not a civic organization, nor is it a charitable institution and as strange as it may seem it is not even a fraternal organization.

Returning to the predicate of this paper we ask ourselves again, exactly what is the mission of Freemasonry? Do we, you and I, honestly understand in a practical way our duty to educate our members to enlightened discipline and basic human happiness? We routinely state Freemasonry is "A System of Morality veiled in Allegory and illustrated by Symbols." Do we understand this often quoted definition and more importantly do we truly understand its meaning?

Masonry although often misunderstood was not created to simply replicate the simple principles of conduct that any man must have before we consider him for admission into the Brotherhood. Although the key words in the definition are a "System of Morality," it is not the "morality" that can, be simply mirrored. "No" It is the "system". The systemic character of Freemasonry is clearly demonstrated by our unique method of initiation conveyed to and taught to the initiate by means of our ritual.

The word "Morality" has been defined by Masonic philosophers as merely a mindset for "The search for truth and spiritual contemplation" as it affects our actions or conduct. However it is the "System", the "Ritual" and the understanding of its meaning that manifests the principles and objectives of our Spiritual Brotherhood.

If we truly understand and are willing to accept that all truth is intrinsically moral, we have established the predicate of the Mystery of Freemasonry. Remember if you will, as an initiate you were informed that truth is a divine attribute and the foundation of every virtue. Thus, in the pursuit of spiritual truth that is "the system" the transformation we acquire the virtues that are themselves the basis of all morality. It is the base principle of all enlightened thought.

Too often however, the explanation or the meaning of a particular lesson or thought is absent from the ritual. What this often repeated occurrence should teach us is "Never accept ritual as sacred." In order for Ritual to have meaning and truly affect our lives Ritual must be challenged and explored. There is a charge implicit in the title of "Master Mason" that imposes upon each of us the mandate to study and teach the Ritual.

In many Lodges we have seen the transformative character of ritual simply decline and much of the degree work has become mere fraternal ceremonial" Rights of Passage". The result is that too many newly made Masons and some elder brothers possess the title "Master Mason" in name only and do not understand the great weight of responsibility set upon them to preserve, protect and teach the great Masonic truths. There was a day when to teach and instruct was a highly respected Badge of Honor, however today we fail at the greatest responsibility of Masonic scholarship if we do not accept this responsibility and teach our Brethren, especially the newly made brothers, and prevent the slide of our Brotherhood into mediocrity.

I believe that it is simply a matter of membership apathy that in general the Institution of Freemasonry has basically failed it members. The constituent Lodges and I believe even Grand Lodges have failed to provide the instruction and guidance so necessary for the continued spiritual development of the individual Mason. The use of allegory and symbol requires the individual Mason to labor to interpret and apply lessons that underlie these metaphorical modes of expression.

Our Louisiana history is unique with its historical past is rooted in the Scottish Rite and its Ritual. The 1811 Grand Consistory chartered out of the Supreme Council of Jamaica and the roster of members of Perfect Union Lodge #1 which Lodge initiated the call in 1812 for a Grand Lodge in Louisiana for example were a mirror of each other.

This is relevant because I do believe that the Philosophy of Freemasonry is clearly found and taught in the principal themes of the Scottish Rite Degrees and form the basis for our Louisiana traditions. The Ritual teaches us how we should treat others with the same respect that we want for ourselves. The Rite teaches us how to take our life experience to a new level of freedom through intelligent self-disciplined. It gives us the tools to discover who we are so that we can know what makes us happy as individuals. The Rite teaches that the measure of a man is not defined by Race, Color or Religious creeds rather by the content of his heart. In life it is the personal journey we make to our own happiness that is most important. It is upon this principle that we begin to understand and live the philosophy of our brotherhood.

The Symbolic Degrees of the Scottish Rite teach us that Ignorance, Falsehood and Ambition, and constitute the three assassins, were not executed as in the Preston Webbor or York Rite Ritual. These negative human characteristics are ever present impediments to personal advancement and collectively a menace to the orderly advancement of man.

The Degrees of the Lodge of Perfection show us that perfection is attainable only when we understand it is our spiritual side that must be in control of our lives.

The Degrees of the Council of Kadosh' teach us how to function in the world. We are taught to release ourselves from those concerns which bind us or hold us back from the realization of our own happiness.

In the Degrees of the Consistory, we receive an admonition that although we have been enlightened or have understanding, we must always self-reflect to make sure we're not doing the right thing for the wrong reasons. We assess what we know, reflect on where did these ideas come from; we examine our link to the past, and we know these things are true because they have always been true.

The Scottish Rite is an enlightened and enlightening educational experience. It was created and exists for one reason – to develop a profoundly mature, compassionate self-disciplined dynamic individual. The fellowship of learning and being together as men, I am sure everyone will agree is good. However the purpose and objective of the Rite clearly is not just for the good times.

Our personal quest for meaning, for insight into life, personal awareness and spiritual development constitutes the objective worth of a man because that is truly the measure of our Spiritual Brotherhood and its journey to personal fulfillment. So when the knock comes at our inner door and men thirst for our secret, personal development is what they should expect of the Rite because that is precisely what the Rite is. If we develop this mindset then we can begin to grow again individually and collectively as a brotherhood.

In its most simple form this is the mystery to which our young people are drawn looking for personal fulfillment and happiness for their life. Our spiritual brotherhood can be the vehicle that assists in their transformation to their own personal enlightenment. Only through Masonic enlightened education can this be achieved.

Indeed, the Masonic Fraternity is more than just another good time. It is the enjoyment of individual hope and insight and change – which leads to fulfillment and happiness in the reality of here and now! It is my sincere belief that this is truly the revealed Mystery of Freemasonry.

The Use and Symbolism of Color in Masonry

by Frank C. Higgins

THE subject of color in connection with Masonry is one which has received very little attention from students, in the past, but it is nevertheless one which is susceptible to some extremely fascinating speculations and, to the writer's notion, deserves greater attention than has hitherto been accorded it.

In Symbolic Masonry we encounter reference to but three, the alternating black and white of the Mosaic pavement denoting the "dual principle"; the pure white of the Lily and the Blue color attributed to the Lodge and the Heavens which it is said to imitate in certain particulars. From the latter consideration we derive various notes of blue in lodge regalia and decorations. The Green of the Acacia, though not dwelt upon, supplies the final note on Immortality.

In Capitular Masonry, the prevailing color is Red and much weight is given to the colors of the four Veils, respectively Scarlet, Blue, Purple and White, which are self-evidently representations of those employed in the Tabernacle and subsequent Temples of Israel. Red is the color of Vulcan, god of Fire, whom the Jews called Tubal-Cain and whose number is 9, or 3 times 3.

If we are willing to accept the theory that in the original intention of the sequence of Masonic degrees, "Symbolic" Masonry was to represent the birth, education or development and final test of the perfected soul, and "Capitular" Masonry to symbolize the return of the liberated soul to the source of its being, we shall have no difficulty, whatsoever, in assimilating the presence of these colors in Lodge and Chapter, as indicated, with the ancient Semitic philosophy, in which Old Testament Theology and, consequently, Masonry, had its rise.

The old Chaldean cosmogony, which impressed the Egyptian, Phoenician and Hebrew cults alike, regarded the Soul as a spark of the Divinity, precipitated to Earth, through the spheres of the Seven planets and the Zones of the Four Elements, gathering in the course of its journey, its mental, moral and spiritual attributes from the first group and its physical elements from the second.

The original King Solomon's Temples were the Zigurrats of Salmannu Sar* (Shalmanesar) of which the seven stepped or staged

Temple of Bel at Borsippa, the trans-Euphratean suburb of Babylon, was, perhaps, the leading example. They were square edifices, like a nest of seven boxes, one above the other, on a diminishing scale and joined by outer staircases. Beginning with Saturn the most distant and slowest of the planets to make a complete circuit of the ecliptic, they responded to the correct sequence of the heavenly bodies in question, as known to the ancients, and had attributed to them the colors of the spectrum, in the order of their refrangibility.

The lowermost or Saturn stage was, however, colored black, the next or Jupiter stage was Orange colored, the Mars stage Red, the Sun stage gold, the Venus stage pale yellow, that of Mercury blue, and that of the Moon silver. Blue is therefore the color universally symbolic of Hermes and the Hermetic philosophy on which Freemasonry is based.

Each of these stories was a temple to the presiding god of the Planet it represented and a school of the science attributed to it. Thus the final stage in the education of the neophyte was in the "Blue" edifice, prior to his admission to the uppermost or, by reason of the peculiar construction of the Temple, middle chamber, which was the observatory of the Priest Astronomers and Astrologers, who were the interpreters of the will of the gods to mankind and the direct servitors of their divine messenger Nebo, Mercury or Hermes.

The Hebrews in their re-fashioning of the Chaldean cult, substituted the imagery of Jacob's seven stepped ladder, which figure the Egyptians were also familiar with, as evidenced by the numerous little seven stepped ladder amulets found in their sarcophagi and, later, in Roman graves. The Veils of the Temples were clearly symbolical of the elemental Zones. Water, Fire, Air and Earth, in Hebrew respectively Iammim, Nour, Rouach and Iebeschah, the initials of which words, "I. N. R. I.," having the numerical value of 10, 50, 200, 10, or 270, gave the cabalistic number of incarnation, founded upon the nine months, of thirty days each, of human gestation and which was also the number of the identified Osiris and Horus, among the Egyptians; the hypotenuse of a right-angle of 162 by 216.

Red stood for the element Fire, Blue for Air, White for Earth, and Purple for Water, the latter, presumably, because purple color was derived from a shell fish, the murex Purpurea of the Tyrians. Their signs were the Lion, Eagle, Bull and Man of Masonic heraldry. The

Egyptians, who manufactured colored glass and must have made experiments with light, observing that red and green produced black, made these three colors representative of the J, V. and H. of their secret Supreme Being, HUHI, who was none other than our mighty Jehovah. Alternating stripes of Red, Black, Green, Black, standing for the Tetragrammaton, being the chief characteristic of the Apron worn by the celebrating Hierophants of the Mysteries of Isis. In their requisitions for Architects to construct their sacred edifices the Hebrews always specified that they be workers in the four symbolic colors and the symbolic metals which also belong to the planetary septenary quoted.

Bezaleel and Aholiab, builders of the Tabernacle in the Wilderness, were "filled with wisdom of heart to execute all manner of work of the engraver, and of the designing weaver and of the embroiderer in blue, and in purple and in scarlet yarn and in linen thread."

The gold, silver and copper employed were respectively sacred to the Sun, Moon and Planet Venus, while the Onyx stone and Shittim or Acacia wood, so lavishly employed, were symbols of the planet Mercury, which, to them, became the "Angel of the Lord," Raphael.

The celebrated Tyrian Architect, builder of King Solomon's Temple, is likewise described as skillful to work in gold, in silver, in copper and in iron, in stone, in wood, in purple, in blue, in fine linen and in crimson, and also to execute any manner of engraving— again a list of symbolic materials embracing the metals of the Sun, Moon, Venus and Mars, the last two indicative of the physical qualities of Attraction and Repulsion, which engender Vibration and which Science is even now identifying as the great cosmic energy.

In the book of Kings the Tyrian Architect is called "Hirm" and in the book of Chronicles "Churam," but there is no doubt of them being the same individual. It will be recollected that Uri, the father of Bezaleel, is described as a "Son of Chur," which was Chr-Mse, "Son of Horus," the origin of the name "Hermes." The name Churam is the Egyptian Horus-Ammon, the name of the Month of the Ram, in which the Hebrews celebrated their Passover but which the Jews called Abib. (Now called Nisan.)

It is no stretch of imagination whatever to attach the surname Abib to the Hirm of "Kings" as a substitute for the Churam Abi of "Chronicles," when we are again confronted with 5, 10, 200, 40, 1, 2,

10, 2, or 270, the very number of Osiris-Horus we have already referred to.

Many Egyptian sculptures show the figures of Priests holding before the Monarch or the gods, purifying offerings of Fire and Water, the elements of which it was said the Earth had been created and by which it would be destroyed. If, finally, a most delightful theory may be advanced, we would (in our recognition of the advancement of the ancient Seers in many branches of Art and Science which we have only tardily come to justly credit them with), like to presume that part of the universal adoration of Light as the dwelling place of the Deity and the primordial source of substance employed in material creation, consisted in an appreciation of color, as a property of light.

We are perfectly satisfied, that the seven prismatic colors were recognized in the earliest ages of the civilized World. We know that the ancients were acquainted with the manufacture of glass and that in possession of this latter substance, they could scarcely avoid something which is constantly occurring to the astonishment of children, handling glass or crystal in the sunlight, the production of the colors of the rainbow. Why, then, were four colors only selected for the symbols of Matter and the Veils, representing the Elements, by our ancient Brethren? All scientists have heard of Wollaston's celebrated experiment, performed in 1801 for the purpose of discovering the ultimate composition of light. We quote the language of his paper in the Philosophical Transactions of the Royal Society of Great Britain in 1802. He says:

> "I cannot conclude my observations on the dispersion of light without remarking that the colors, into which a beam of white light is separable by refraction, appear to me to be neither seven, as they are usually seen in the Rainbow, nor reducible by any means, that I can find to three, as some persons have conceived, but that by employing a very narrow pencil of light four primary divisions of the prismatic spectrum may be seen with a degree of distinctness, that I believe has not been described or observed before."

"If a beam of daylight be admitted into a dark room by a crevice, 1-20 of an inch broad, and received by the eye at a distance of ten or twelve feet through a prism of flint glass, free from veins, held near the eye, the beam is seen separated into the four following colors only: Red, a yellowish Green (which might pass as a muddy White), Blue and Violet." The very diagram employed by Wollaston to illustrate this experiment, a human eye viewing the four ultimate colors through a triangular prism, suggests above all things the notion of the all-seeing eye, in the Triangle, viewing His Creation as a compound of the four elements, as those only known to and symbolized by ancient Science. The student desirous of pursuing this subject farther will find extensive notes on the Biblical and Classical employment of the seven prismatic colors, in Mackey's Encyclopedia of Freemasonry, which detail various ancient conceptions in an interesting manner.

*Literally, "King Solomon," also paraphrased by the Hebrews, Sar Salom, "Prince of Peace."

The Doctrine of the Balance

by Joseph Fort Newton

READERS of Albert Pike will recall the stately pages with which Morals and Dogma closes, setting forth, in a manner unforgetable, the Doctrine of the Balance. Many had taught this truth before time out of mind, no one more impressively than the man whom Pike was richly indebted,[1] but his exposition is none the less his own. With vast labor he brings together his findings, showing that to this result the wisdom of the ages runs, what the sages have thought equally with what the mystics have dreamed. Always it is a triad, suggested by the ancient idea of the number Three, the singular, the dual and the plural, the odd and even added, and the great emblem of the Triangle—symbol of perfection. It is seen in all Masonic symbolism, from end to end and at every step of the Mystic quest for the secret which every Mason is seeking.

Eloquently, and with every variation of emphasis and illustration, he lays the matter before us, carrying it into all the fields of human activity and aspiration. Sympathy and Antipathy, Attraction and Repulsion, Fate and Freedom, each a fact of life and a force of nature, are contraries alike in the universe and in the soul of man, wherein we see eternity in miniature. As the earth is held in its orbit by the action of opposing forces, so truth is made up of two opposite propositions, as peace lies in the union of motion and rest, and harmony is the fruit of seeming war. Here he finds the solution of the problem of the One and the Many, of the Infinite and the Finite, of Unity amidst Manifoldness: the principle of the Balance, the secret of the universal equilibrium:

"Of that Equilibrium in the Deity, between the Infinite Divine Wisdom and the Infinite Divine Power; from which result the Stability of the Universe, the unchangeableness of the Divine Law, and the Principles of Truth, Justice, and Right which are a part of it; . . Of that Equilibrium also, between the Infinite Divine Justice and the Infinite Divine Mercy, the result of which is the Infinite Divine Equity, and the Moral Harmony or Beauty of the Universe. By it the endurance of created and imperfect natures in the presence of a Perfect Deity is made possible; . .

Of that Equilibrium between Necessity and Liberty, between the action of the Divine Omnipotence and the Free-will of man, by which vices and base actions, and ungenerous thoughts and words are crimes and wrongs, justly punished by the law of cause and consequence, though nothing in the universe can happen or be done contrary to the will of God; and without which co-existence of Liberty and Necessity, of Free-will in the creature and Omnipotence in the Creator, there could be no religion, nor any law of right and wrong, or merit or demerit, nor any justice in human punishments or penal laws.

And, finally, of that Equilibrium, possible in ourselves, and which Masonry incessantly labors to accomplish in its Initiates, and demands of its Adepts and Princes (else unworthy of their titles between the Spiritual and Divine and the Material and human in man; between the Intellect, Reason, and Moral Sense on one side, and the Appetites and Passions on the other, from which result the Harmony and Beauty of a well-regulated life."[2] And so on, through a passage of singular elevation both of language and of thought, we are led by an ancient truth which becomes a vision in the mind of a nobler thinker. My design is not to add to his exposition, but to apply it with emphasis and illustration, if so that it may be brought home to our "business and bosom" and be of real service to us in the life which we live together, and in the life which each must live alone. For it is the high service of Masonry that it puts a man in the straight path which the wisest of the race have walked, leading him midway between the falsehood of extremes, and bringing the highest teaching of the past to the uses of the present. After all, how to live is the one matter; and he is wise who joins the goodly Shakespeare gospel of Courage, Sanity and Pity with that other Gospel of Faith, Hope, and Love. Every man will need all the aid he can get, unless he be content, as no real man can be, to live in the world as a mere looker-on at a drama in which others are actors,

"In God's vast house a curious guest, Seeing how all works take their flight." From bottom to top life is a contradiction and a paradox, and the beginning of wisdom is to know that fact and adjust ourselves to it. Light and darkness, heat and cold, mind and matter, fate and free-will, asceticism and indulgence, socialism and anarchy, dogmatism and doubt, reason and authority—no man may ever hope to live long enough, much less to think deeply enough, to harmonize these paradoxes. The way of wisdom is to accept both facts in each case, as the Two Pillars of a Temple of Truth, and walk between them into the hush of the holy place. Either one, without the other, is only a half-truth which ends in perversion, if not in insanity, turning the hearty, wholesome, clear seeing spirit of manhood into the pitiful narrowness and hardness of a bigot or a fanatic.

For example: "All is free- that is false: all is fate—that is false. All things are free and fated— that is true."[3] It is possible to make an argument in behalf of fatalism so freezing that one is left with the feeling that he is no more responsible for his thoughts and acts, than he is for the shape of his head and the color of his eyes. Having listened to such an argument, each of us may say, as Dr. Johnson did,[4] "I know I am free, and that's the end on it." On the other side, one can present a thesis in proof of the freedom of man so convincing that fate seems a fiction. Both are true, and the great truth consists of two opposites which are not contradictory—that it is the Fate of man to be Free if he fights for it, approves himself worthy of it, uniting his will with the Will of the Master of the World! Otherwise, we men are slaves journeying downward "to the dust of graves," slaves of greed and passion and a fatal folly.

Asceticism is one extreme, indulgence another. One would repress every natural instinct in behalf of a pale, wan purity; the other would follow every fancy, driven hither and yon by every gust of passion, at the mercy of every caprice. Between the two lies temperance, keeping the balance between two absurdities, making a right use of everything, and abusing nothing; its motto the wise words of the old Greeks, "In nothing too much." Socialism seems to hold that the State is everything, the Individual nothing—or at best only a cog in a vast machine, an atom in an indistinguishable blur. Anarchy makes the State nothing, and the Individual everything—each a law unto himself, and chaos at the end. Between the two lies the way of wise government in which "Freedom slowly broadens down from precedent to precedent," or grows gladly up from the life of a just and intelligent people. There are certain things which every man must surrender in behalf of the common good, and other things which it were a sin to abdicate, the while a shifting, zig-zag line runs between dividing the man from the mass.

By the same token, in religion Dogmatism affirms everything, makes a map of the Infinite, and an atlas of Eternity, so certain is it of things whereof no man knoweth. It talks of God as if He were a man in the next room. It knows the origin of all things, and the final destiny of humanity. Doubt denies everything, questions the competence of the human mind to know Divine things, leaving us with the assurance that nothing is certain but uncertainty; nothing secure but insecurity. Again it is the doctrine of the balance, as in the natural world peace is found amid the poise of powers. Between dogmatism and doubt is a wise and reverent Faith, which dares to say, "Now we know in part—a tiny part, no doubt—but knowledge is real as far as it goes, and what we know gives us confidence in the vast Unknown. And so we make bold to trust the ultimate decency of things and the veiled kindness of the Father of men, assured that He who has brought us to where we are will lead us to where we ought to be !"

Of this fundamental paradox of life the Cross is the symbol. Older than Christianity, as old, almost, as human life, it is the supreme symbol of the race. When man first emerged from the "old dark backward and abysm of time," he had a cross in his hand. Where he got it, what he meant by it, many may conjecture but no one knows. The Cross, like life itself, is also a collision and a contradiction—its four arms pointing every whither, making it the great guide-post of free thought. As long as a man keeps his poise, never forgetting the profound paradox at the heart of all high thought, he may think as far and as fast as his mind can go. For many of us, of course, the Cross is hallowed anew and forever by the name of One whose life was a tragedy, whose love was heroic in its gentleness, who wins by "that strange power called weakness," whose character is the sovereign wonder of the world, and whose spirit is the holiest tradition of humanity.

Since this is so, since the way of sanity, if not of salvation, lies in keeping our balance, why is it that men lose their poise ? No man of us, when he thinks of the days agone, but recalls acts which he not only regrets, but which puzzle him by their strange stupidity. He would give almost as much to be able to understand them as he would to forget them. Why is this so? Shakespeare has much to teach us here, much of abiding profit to remember, if so that we may understand the past and make a better use of the future. He everywhere shows that tragedy is the fruit of treachery, and that treachery has its roots in obsession[5] — some one thing that gets so close to the mind that it can see nothing else, blinds it, preys upon it, making a man first a fanatic, and then, it may be, a criminal. Macbeth was a man of noble nature; his wife was a lovely lady. They became obsessed with ambition for place and power, and to what dark depths of sin and shame that mad blindness led them that terrible tragedy tells us. This lesson, taught so often by our supreme poet, is for each of us, teaching us to keep our poise, and to flee an obsession as a plague. Whatever fastens itself upon the mind, shutting out the light, marring the proportions and perspectives of things, forebodes disaster.

Perhaps it is physical passion. If so, it will turn love into lust and make the world a bawdy-house. It may be political ambition, and a man throws everything to the winds in order to win, forgetting that no office on earth is worth the sacrifice of integrity—and, also, if he wins by trickery he is unfit to hold it. It may be religion. Think of the crimes unspeakable, the brutalities unbelievable, which have been committed by men in a frenzy of fanatical bigotry—dipping their hands in blood and thinking they were doing the will of God ! They were madmen. Plato said that all men are more or less insane, and that the man whom we put in a straight-jacket is only a little more emphatically out of his mind than the rest of us. The more reason, then, why we should keep our poise and walk the quiet way of sanity and charity, in love of God and man.

After this manner we expound the Doctrine of the Balance, as taught by Pike, reminding our Brethren, as we remind ourselves, that the wisdom of life lies in freedom, serenity, and forgiveness, in victory by selfsurrender to the highest laws of life, and that we dare not turn either to the right or the left. By such teaching men become happy and free; in this way we may grow old without being sad, and wise without being cynical; and learn, at last, that everlasting gentleness which is the highest wisdom man may win from the hard facts and the often strange medley of his days. Let us also lay to heart the prayer quoted by Pike:

Him, the ever-living God, be always present in thy mind; for thy mind itself is His likeness, for it, too, is invisible and impalpable, and without form. As He exists forever, so thou also, when thou shalt put off this which is visible and corruptible, shalt stand before Him forever, living and endowed with knowledge."

NOTES

(1) *Eliphas Levi. Digest of his Writings.* translated by A.E. Waite, especially pp. 79-83.
(2) *Morals and Dogma*, pp. 859-60.
(3) *Life of F.W. Robertson*, p. 32, note.
(4) *Life of Johnson*, by Boswell.
(5) *Shakespeare*, by John Masefield.

Masonic Words and Phrases

Edited by Michael R. Poll, PM
Secretary, Louisiana Lodge of Research

FREEMASONRY, when properly understood, is a life-long journey towards self-improvement. By means of presenting certain philosophical truths, the teachings of Freemasonry can offer an opportunity for living a more productive and rewarding life. There is, however, no final examination administered by grand lodges to determine when self-improvement takes place nor any attempt to determine ones level of self-improvement (if such a thing could be measured). Ours is a personal journey down the particular path we choose for ourselves. There is no rule that we must all walk the same path nor any yardstick used to measure our progress against another. The fact is that if one wishes to remain a member of a lodge, but make no attempt towards self-improvement, he may well remain a member of that lodge for life. If, however, one wishes to employ the teachings of Masonry with the goal of personal development, then a proper foundation is necessary.

The first steps to properly understanding the philosophical truths offered by Masonry require an understanding of the medium used to deliver these truths. In our case, this would mean an understanding of our symbols, words, usages and manner of presenting our instructions. By understanding these basic elements, our ways of teaching become clear and we can properly benefit from all that Masonry offers.

The goal of this work is to provide a handy and useful quick reference guide to many of the common words and phrases used in Masonry. While not designed to replace the education a new Mason receives from his instructor, this work can augment any study plan and provide valuable assistance to any Mason. This basic work is designed to be only one of many tools used by the dedicated student during his journey towards self-mastership.

A

Aaron

he was the brother of and "second in command" to Moses, and the first high priest under Mosaic dispensation; he was the founder of the "Aaronic" priesthood.

Aaron's Rod

the rod or staff carried by Aaron, brother of Moses, as a token of his office. The rod miraculously blossomed as evidence of his Divine choice as High Priest. It was afterwards preserved in the Ark of the Covenant.

Abhorrence of Evil

the quality required of all true Masons.

Abif

The "Abif" of Hiram Abif does not appear in the Bible. The word Abi or Abiw or Abiv is translated in the King James version both as "his father" and "my father" - using the word "father" as a term of respect and not as denoting a parent. Hiram, the widow's son of the tribe of Naphtali, was "my father" in the same sense that Abraham was "my father" to members of the tribes of Israel.

The thought that the two syllables are a surname is an error. The legend gains, not loses, in appeal when Abif becomes a title of honor. Just when and how it came into the Masonic terminology is still unknown; it does not appear in the Regis document (oldest of our Constitutions, dated approximately 1390) but does appear - only as one name among many - in the Dowland manuscript of 1550. Apparently the term was not in common use until after the King James Bible (1611) had become familiar in Masonic circles.

The story of Hiram Abif as told in the Masonic tale is not found in the Bible, nor is there any meaning in the word which can be construed as part of the story as Masons tell it, except that of veneration.

Abraham

in the Bible, the first patriarch and progenitor of the Hebrew people. He was the father of Isaac. Abraham was earlier known as Abram, the son of Terah of Ur. His name was changed to Abraham by God. He was noted for his faith, for piety, and for his loyalty to God.

Acacia

any of various often spiny trees or shrubs of the genus *Acacia* in the pea family, having alternate, bi-pinnately compound leaves or leaves represented by flattened leaf-stalks and heads or spikes of small flowers. Also, the Shittim tree. The wood of the Shittim tree is said to have been used for the furniture of the Temple of Solomon. In speculative Masonry, the term is often used as a symbol of the immortality of the soul.

Accepted

In Operative Masonry members were admitted through course of time, and when the Craft had begun to decay, gentlemen who had no intention of doing builders' work, but were interested in the Craft for social, or perhaps for antiquarian reasons, were "accepted" into membership; to distinguish these gentlemen Masons from the Operatives in the membership they were called the "Accepted." After 1717, when the whole Craft was revolutionized into a Fraternity, all members became non-Operatives, hence our use of the word in such phrases as "Free and Accepted Masons."

Accord

to make to conform or agree; bring into harmony. Required of all Masons in the philosophical sense in order to attain true Brotherhood.

Active Member

an active member is one who maintains his membership in a Masonic Lodge by the payment of his lodge dues and who takes part in the work and duties of the Craft. One who fails to do these things may remain a Mason at heart, but deprives himself of the benefits of active membership.

Adam

in the Bible, the first man and the husband of Eve. The name denotes that he was derived from the ground.

Adjournment

to suspend until a later stated time. The Worshipful Master is the most often the sole judge with reference to the adjournment of a Lodge, unless a time is fixed in the lodge bylaws.

Adhering Mason

There was a time in America (early 1800's) when the enemies of Freedom formed an anti-Masonic political party. The issues of the anti-Masons were brought before the people of the United States, and the anti-Masonic party was soundly defeated in a national election. The time, however, was still difficult for many Masons in different areas of the U.S. Those Masons who remained loyal to their lodges and grand lodges were called Adhering Masons. The "Adhering Mason" was then often scorned; now the term is one of honor.

Admonish

to reprove gently, but firmly. One of the most exacting duties in the ethics of Freemasonry is that a Mason should not publicize the faults of a Brother Mason, but shall whisper good, private counsel in his ear. An admonition must be given in the language of brotherly affection, the magic tongue of love, and with the persuasive attitude of "mercy unrestrained."

Adonai

used in Judaism as a spoken substitute for the ineffable name of God. While this proper name is not found in our English Bible, it occurs in several passages of the original Greek and Hebrew texts.

Adoration

the act of worship. A fundamental tenet of Freemasonry is that God is supreme, pre-eminent, and exalted above all creation, and that He alone is to be worshipped. Throughout all of the Degrees and in all of the ritual of Masonry, God is worshipped in adorations which are expressed in both silent and oral prayers.

Adversity

a state of hardship or affliction; misfortune. Freemasonry believes that adversity should be accepted as a test of character and met with courage and prayer. Also, a Mason should go to the aid of a Brother Mason in adversity.

Affiliate

to associate oneself as a subordinate, subsidiary, employee, or member. *Filius* is Latin for son, *filia* for daughter; the prefix "af" is a form of the Latin ad, meaning to add to. To be affiliated means therefore to be adopted into a family as a son or daughter, a meaning that beautifully covers a Mason's relation to their Lodge once they have affiliated with it.

Affirmation

something declared to be true; a positive statement or judgment. Affirmations instead of oaths are entirely inadmissible in Freemasonry.

Age, Lawful

this is the age when a man may apply to join a Masonic Lodge. In many jurisdictions, it is the age of twenty-one (21); in others, it is eighteen (18).

Ahiman Rezon

a book of Masonic law. The Antients' Grand Lodge of England published a Book of Constitutions in 1756, under the title "Ahiman Rezon, or a Help to a Brother." Eight editions were published in all before the Union of the two Grand Lodges in England in 1813. The title "Ahiman Rezon" was brought to America and used by several Grand Lodges; it is still the title of the books of law in Pennsylvania and South Carolina.

Aid of Deity

a fundamental principle of Freemasonry as illustrated in David's intercession for Solomon for the task of building the Temple.

Alarm

The Latin for weapons, or arms, was *arma*. Our "art" and "article" came from the same root, art meaning something originally made by the use of the arms, hands and fingers. The English "alarm" goes back directly to the Italian *alle arme*, and ultimately to the Latin ad *arma* so that "alarm" means "to arms, signifying that something has happened of possible danger. A knock at the Lodge door is so named because it calls for alertness, lest one unworthy be permitted to enter.

Allegiance

A Mason's first allegiance is to God, second to his family, then to his country and then to his Lodge.

Allegory

The Greeks called a place of public assembly agora; from this they built the word *agoreuein*, meaning speak, in the sense of addressing the public. When to this is added alias, meaning another, the compound gives us our "allegory," which is the speaking about one thing in the terms of something else. In Masonry we have the allegory of Solomon's Temple, of a journey, of the legend of a martyr builder, etc., in each case the acting and describing of one thing being intended to refer to some other thing. For example, the building of Solomon's Temple is described, not for the purpose of telling how that structure was erected, but to suggest how men may work together in brotherliness at a common task.

All-Seeing Eye

A perpetual and permanent symbol in the Lodge and work of Freemasonry, signifying the omnipresence and omniscience of God.

Almsgiving

helping the poor; a cornerstone of charity.

Altar

Alt, in Latin, referred to height, preserved in our "altitude;" this root appeared in *altare*, literally meaning a "high place." In primitive religion it was a common practice to make sacrifices, or conduct worship, on the top of a hill, or high platform, so that "altar" came to be applied to any stone, post, platform, or other elevation used for such purposes. The altar holds the central place in the Lodge room of Freemasons. Lying on the altar is the Holy bible, the principal Light of Masons, which is open during the work of the Lodge. Here, candidates voluntarily kneel and assume the obligations of the several Degrees.

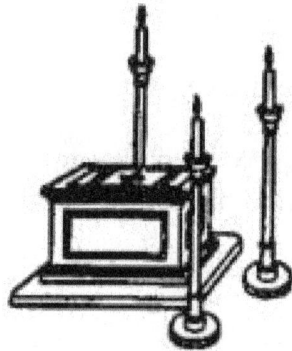

Amen

used at the end of a prayer or a statement to express assent or approval. An expression by which one person confirms the word of another and expresses his wish for the success of that word. Following "Amen," Masons often employ the literal rendering of the word, "So mote it be."

Anchor

In those Degrees of Masonry where the ceremonies and instructions relate to life and death, man's journey over the sea of life is symbolized by Noah's Ark, and the hope of immortality and a safe landing in the haven of eternal security is symbolized by the anchor.

Anger

a strong feeling of displeasure or hostility. The tenets of Freemasonry teach its members to avoid and to subdue every element of ire and wrath, or enraged emotions and malicious emotions and sentiments.

Angle

the inclination of two lines meeting in a point. Angles are of three kinds-acute, obtuse, and right angles. The right angle, or the angle of 90 degrees, is the principal one recognized in Freemasonry.

Apprentice

one bound by legal agreement to work for another for a specific amount of time in return for instruction in a trade, art, or business. In Latin *apprehendre* meant to lay hold of a thing in the sense of learning to understand it, the origin of our "apprehend." This became contracted into *apprendre* and was applied to a young man beginning to learn a trade. The latter term came into circulation among European languages and, through the Operative Masons, gave us our "apprentice," that is, one who is beginning to learn Masonry. An "Entered Apprentice" is one whose name has been entered in the books of the Lodge having received the first degree of Masonry.

Apron

The Operative Masons wore a leather apron out of necessity; when the craft became speculative this garment, so long identified with building work, was retained as the badge of Masons. Hence, in the First Degree of Freemasonry, the initiate is presented with the pure white lambskin apron as a reminder of that purity of life and rectitude of conduct which is so essentially necessary to his gaining admission into the Celestial Lodge above where the Supreme Architect of the Universe resides forever. This apron becomes his permanent property as the "badge of a Freemason." As he advances in Masonry, he may receive other aprons of varying types, but never one that equals this first one in emblematic significance and Masonic value.

Arch, Holy Royal

Job compares Heaven to an arch supported by pillars. This is, of course, allegorical, even as is the name "Holy Royal Arch" degree in Masonry. The pillars which support the arch are emblematical of Wisdom and Strength; the former denoting the wisdom of the Supreme Architect, and the latter the stability of the universe.

Architecture

The five orders of architecture recognized in Freemasonry are Doric, Ionic, Corinthian, Tuscan and Composite. The Doric order represents the West; the Corinthian Column represents the South. The Gothic, or pointed style of architecture, was intimately connected with the Middle Ages, over which Freemasonry maintained exclusive control.

Ark of the Covenant

The Ark of the Covenant was a chest originally constructed according to specific instructions given to Moses by God, and was the only article placed in the Holy of Holies in the Temple. Within the Ark were placed the two tables or tablets of stone on which the Ten Commandments were engraved, Aaron's baton which had budded as a token of his divine appointment to the office of High Priest, and a pot of manna.

Artificers

Tubal-cain was the first notable artificer mentioned in history. The best available of these master craftsmen were employed in the building of the Temple.

Arts, Parts and Points

these terms are used in the mysteries of Masonry. Arts represents the knowledge or things made known; Parts, the degrees into which Masonry is divided; and Points, the rules and usages of Masonry.

Arts and Sciences

Freemasonry recognizes the seven principal arts and sciences as: Grammar, Rhetoric, Logic, Arithmetic, Geometry, Music and Astronomy.

Asher

in the Bible, a son of Jacob and the forebear of one of the tribes of Israel. In the tribal blessings promised to him, his tribe was to enjoy richness and royal dainties. Hence, entrusting the Masonic initiates with the mysteries of the Order is symbolized by the tribe of Asher.

Ashlar

a squared block of building stone. The Latin *assis* was a board or plank; in the diminutive form, *assula*, it meant a small board, like a shingle, or a chip. In early English this became *asheler* and was used to denote a stone in the rough as it came from the quarries. The Operative Masons called such a stone a "rough ashlar," and when it had been shaped and finished for its place in the wall they called it a "perfect ashlar." An Apprentice is a rough ashlar, because unfinished, whereas a Master Mason should be a perfect ashlar, because he has been shaped for his place in the organization of the Craft.

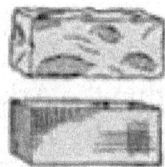

Ask, Seek, Knock

The applicant for membership in Freemasonry Asks for acceptance, Seeks for Light, and Knocks for initiation.

Atheism

the doctrine that there is no God. No atheist can become a

Mason in a lodge recognized by most jurisdictions. Every candidate must confess faith in God before crossing the threshold of the Lodge. This confession is an essential element in all the work of a Masonic Lodge.

Audi, Vide, Tace

these Latin words form the motto often found on Masonic medals and documents. They mean: *Hear, See, Be Silent.*

B

Backbiting

slandering a brother in his absence.

Badge of a Mason

see Apron.

Balloting

Balloting on the acceptance or rejection of a candidate is secret. Small round white balls and black cubes are used in the voting. White balls elect; black cubes reject. In casting the ballot, all lodge members are required to base their ballot on personal knowledge, information of the committee on investigation, and reputed character of

the candidate. Under no circumstances are members to allow themselves to be influenced by personal likes and dislikes of the candidate or by a spirit of prejudice or revenge.

Every member of the lodge is required to vote conscientiously for the good of the Order and in Brotherly consideration of the applicant.

Banishment

to drive away or expel. The practice of Freemasonry in banishing from its membership unworthy persons is fully sustained by Biblical authority and practice.

Barefoot

The removal of one or both shoes has been for many hundreds of years a token of reverence and a symbol of yielding one's self to the control and sovereignty of another.

Battery

In Masonry, a battery is normally specific raps of the gavels by the officers or claps of the hands by the members. A battery is a formal salute or Grand Honors; given in one form in public, in another in a tiled lodge.

Beauty

Operative Masonry has as its chief objective beauty and symmetry in architecture in building of King Solomon's Temple; speculative Masonry emphasizes the beauty of character and the virtues of true manhood.

Beehive

Among the ancients, the bee-hive was a symbol of an obedient people and an emblem of system-atized industry. Hence, Freema-sonry has adopted the beehive as a symbol on industry — a virtue stressed in ritual and by lectures.

Benediction

an invocation of Divine blessing. A Lodge must never be closed without a solemn prayer.

Benevolence

an inclination to perform kind, charitable acts. Freemasonry is not to be classified as a benevolent institution; but the disposi-tion and practice of benevolence is strongly stressed by the Fra-ternity.

Bible

masons accept this Book and believe in it as the Law of God, as the Great Light of Freemasonry. It is an open Book on the altar during all work of the Lodge, and certain appropriate passages are used for the different Degrees.

Bigotry

intolerance toward those of different creeds, races, nation-alities or religious affiliations. Bigotry has no place in Freema-sonry.

Blue

Blue is the accepted color of Freemasonry. As the color of the vault of Heaven, which embraces and covers the entire earth, it is to a Mason the symbol of universal friendship and benevolence. The name "Blue Lodge" or "Blue House" designates the Symbolic Lodge in which the first three degrees are conferred.

Boaz

in the Bible, the husband of Ruth. Signified by "strength," Boaz is the name of the left-hand pillar that stood on the porch of King Solomon's Temple, and adopted into speculative Masonry because of its symbolic meaning. It was broken to pieces by the Babylonians and carried to the city of Babylon.

Book of Constitutions
Guarded by the Tiler's Sword

reminds us that we should be ever watchful and guarded in our thoughts, words, and actions, particularly when before the enemies of Masonry; ever bearing in remembrance those truly Masonic virtues, silence and circumspection.

Book Of The Law

this is another name for the Holy Bible.

Brass

this metal was used extensively in the building of the Temple.

Brazen

made of brass

Brother

this word is one of the oldest, as it is one of the most beautiful, in any language. No one knows where or when it originated, but it is certain that it existed in the Sanskrit, in a form strikingly similar to that used by us. In Greek, it was *phrater*, in the Latin *frater*, whence our "fraternal" and "fraternalism." It has always meant men from the same parents, or men knit by very close blood ties. When associated with *initiation*, which has the general meaning of "being born into," one can see how appropriate is its use in Freemasonry. All of us have, through initiation in our "mother" Lodges, been born into a Masonry and therefore we are "brothers," and that which holds us together in one great family is the "Mystic Tie," the Masonic analogue of the blood tie among kinsmen.

Brotherly Love

Freemasonry recognizes the Divine requirement that godly men love their neighbors and that this love should be for all mankind. Emphasis is placed upon the privilege and duty of special love for members of the Fraternity. There are certain bonds and obligations in Freemasonry, which are fulfilled only in the spirit of true brotherhood.

Building of the Temple

Speculative Masonry has evolved indirectly from the organization of the workmen in the construction of Solomon's Temple and the union of operative masons who labored on that notable and Holy Building. Much of the subject of the ritual is traced directly back to the building of the Temple.

Burial

From time immemorial, Freemasons have given special attention to the interment of their dead, and the proper burial of a Brother Mason is regarded as a sacred and binding duty. Solemn, beautiful and profoundly meaningful burial rites and ceremonies are provided for deceased Brothers where such are requested by the Brother himself or by members of his family.

C

Cabletow

a compound word of Masonic coinage combining cable (a rope) and tow (a rope for pulling). Symbolically, it represents the covenant or first ties by which all Masons are bound.

Cable's Length

a maritime unit of length; about 100 fathoms or 600 feet. Can also mean the limit of a Mason's ability to do something.

Candidate

Among Romans it was the custom for a man seeking office to wear a shining white robe. Since the name for such a color was *candidus* (whence our "candid"), the office seeker came to be called candidate. In our ceremonies the custom is reversed: the candidate is clothed after his election instead of before.

Capital

the top part of a pillar or column.

Cardinal

of foremost importance; paramount. In Masonry we have "cardinal points" and "cardinal virtues." The Greeks had *kradan*, meaning, "swing on," and the Romans had *cardo*, meaning "hinge." The roots mean that on which a thing swings, or hinges, on which a thing depends or hangs, therefore anything that is of fundamental or pivotal, importance. A member of the Sacred College of the Roman Church is a Cardinal because of the importance of his office, which ranks next in dignity to that of the Pope. The cardinal points of the compass are those from which are determined all other points, north, east, south, west; the cardinal virtues are those which are fundamental to all other virtues.

Cardinal Points

East represents Wisdom; West, strength; South, beauty; North, darkness.

Cardinal Virtues

these are the principal virtues of which all others hinge. As set forth in the Entered Apprentice Degree, they are Temperance, Fortitude, Prudence and Justice.

Cedars of Lebanon

Among the finest and most perfect cedars ever known in history of the world were those of Lebanon. Through his alliance with Hiram, King of Tyre, Solomon secured cedars from these mountains for use in construction of the Temple.

Ceremony

The Latin *caerimonia* referred to a set of formal acts having a sacred, or revered, character. A ceremony differs from a merely formal act in that it has a religious significance; a formality becomes a ceremony only when it is made sacred. A "ceremony" may be individual, or may involve only two persons; a "rite" is more public, and necessarily involves many. An "observance" is public, as when the whole nation observes Memorial Day. A "Master of Ceremonies" is one who directs and regulates forms, rites and ceremonies.

Chambers

In the erection of King Solomon's Temple, a series of chambers were built on three sides of the Temple (north, south and west). This building against the wall of the Temple were three stories high (30 feet). These small chambers were used for Temple offices and for storage.

Charge

Among the most beautiful and forceful features of the work of Masonry are the solemn and exacting charges given to the candidate as he advances from one Degree to another.

Charity

The three great cardinal virtues are Faith, Hope and Love. Charity as an act of genuine, heart-felt love is so closely related that it is sometimes employed in the place of Love, and is regarded as one of the three great cardinal virtues. The Greeks had a word, *charisma*, meaning a gift, and a number of words from the same root, variously suggesting rejoicing, gladness. The Latins had a similar word, *carus*, and meaning *dear*, possibly connected with am or, signifying love. From these roots came *grace*, meaning a

free, unbought gift, as in the theological phrase, "the grace of God," and "charity." Strictly speaking, charity is an act done freely, and spontaneously out of friendship, not as a civic duty and grudgingly, as is sometimes the case in public charity. The Masonic use of the word is much nearer this original sense, for a Mason extends relief to a needy brother not as a duty, but out of caring.

Charter

In Latin *charta* was a paper, a card, a map; in Medieval Latin this became an official paper, as in the case of "Magna Charta." Our "chart" and "card" are derived from the same root. A Masonic charter is the written paper, or instrument, empowering a group of brethren to act as a Lodge.

Chasity

remaining pure in sexual relations.

Cipher

a reference book, printed by the Grand Lodge, containing much of the Masonic Ritual. It is encoded, and available to Master Masons with the permission of their Grand Lodge.

Circumambulation

to walk around something, especially as part of a ritual. In Masonic terminology this is the technical name of that ceremony in which the candidate walks around the Lodge. The word 4 is derived from the Latin prefix *cireum*, meaning "around," and *ainbulare*, meaning "walk," whence our ambulate, ambulatory, etc.; a circumambulation is therefore a walking around. In ancient religions and mysteries the worshippers walked around an altar; imitating the movements of the sun; this became known as circumambulation, and is the origin of our own ceremony.

Circumscribe

to draw a line around; encircle by the compasses; symbolic of the boundary line of Masonic conduct. To limit in range of activity definitely and clearly.

Citizenship

Perhaps no institution or organization has contributed more to good citizenship than Freemasonry. Democratic principles, good government, freedom of conscience and civic liberty have always been championed by Masons. Many of the world's great patriots and statesmen of all nations have been members of the Fraternity. Loyalty to one's government, faithfulness in all the duties of citizenship, and active support of public institutions are demanded throughout all the rituals of Freemasonry.

Clad

to cover as if with clothing.

Clandestine

In Anglo Saxon *helan* meant something hidden, or secret, a meaning preserved in "conceal;" "hell," the hidden place, is from the same word. Helan descended' from the Latin celare, hide; and on this was built the Latin clandestinus, secret, hidden, furtive. In English, clandestine, thus derived, came to mean a bad secret, one that must be indulged in furtively. A secret may be innocent; it is merely something done without the knowledge of others, and nothing is more common; but a clandestine act is one done in such a way as to elude observation. *Clandestine Masonry* has come to be regarded as a kind of irregular and unlawful secret society falsely claiming to be Masonic.

Clay Ground

the use of this term in Masonic work is based on the fact that a special clay found only in the Jordan Valley was used in casting the two great pillars, called Boaz and Jachin, which stood before the Great Porch of Solomon's Temple. This same clay was also used for casting ornaments and vessels used in the Temple.

Cleft

to split with or as if with a sharp instrument. An opening made by a crack or crevice; a hollow between two parts.

Clods of the Valley

this term is used in Masonic ritual in its Biblical meaning and signifies the sweetness of rest for the dead of the Lord.

Clothing

It has always been the custom among all peoples for designated officers, leaders, and people of rank to wear special regalia or a particular type of clothing which indicates a person's official position. Based on this custom and upon Biblical examples, and for reasons of dignity and beauty, Masons follow this practice.

In Masonic usage the meaning is much narrower and more technical; a Mason is clothed when he wears the apron and the emblem of his rank. The apron and gloves are also employed as symbols, though gloves have pretty much fallen into disuse in American Masonry.

Column

Three columns are employed to signify the supports of a Lodge; the columns of Wisdom, Strength and Beauty. The Greeks called the top or summit of anything kolophon; in Latin culmen had a similar meaning; from these origins come our culmination; excelsior, colophon, colonnade, colonel, and climax appears to he closely related to it. A "column" is a cylindrical, or slightly tapering, support; a "pillar" is a rectangular support. Either may stand free or be incorporated into the building fabric. The officers of a Lodge are figured as columns because they are the supports of the official fabric of the Lodge. The Great Pillars are symbolical representations of the two pillars, which stood on the Porch of King Solomon's Temple.

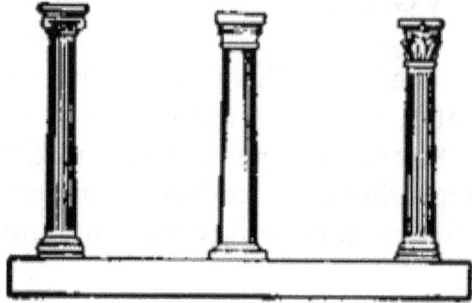

Common Gavel, The

The Common Gavel is an instrument used by operative Masons to break off the rough and superfluous parts of stones, the better to fit them for the builder's use. But we, as Free and Accepted Masons, are taught to make use of it for the more noble and glorious purpose of divesting our hearts and consciences of all the vices and superfluities of life; thereby fitting our minds as living stones for that spiritual building, that house not made with hands, eternal in the heavens.

Communication

A Masonic Lodge meeting is called a "communication" because it dates back to the earliest meaning of the word — the having of things in common, the fellowship of those engaged in a common purpose, governed by a common principle, and participation in common interests and activities.

Masonic communication is also understood to be the sharing of Masonic secrets with those entitled to such secrets. Masonic communication is *not* general, polite conversation with the profane or irregular Masons when no Masonic secrets are shared.

Compasses

The compasses are emblems of virtue, the true and holy measure of a Mason's life and conduct. This is the plural of compass, from the Latin *corn*, meaning "together," and *passus*, meaning a pass, step, way, or route. Contrivance, cunning, encompass, pass, pace derive from the same roots. A circle was once described as a compass because all the steps in making it were "together," that is, of the same distance from the center; and the word, natural transition, became applied to the familiar two-legged instrument for drawing a circle. Some jurisdictions use the word in the singular, as in "square and compass," but the plural form "square and compasses" would appear to he preferable, especially since it immediately distinguishes the working tool from the mariner's compass, with which it might be otherwise confused by the uninformed.

Composite

one of the five orders of architecture, combining the Corinthian and Ionic styles

Consecration

Sacer was the Latin for something set aside as holy. By prefixing *con*, meaning "together," consecrare resulted, the general significance of which was that by adding to some holy object a formal ceremony the object was declared to be holy to the public, and must therefore be treated as such. The ceremony of consecrating a Lodge room is a way of giving notice to the public that it has been dedicated, or set aside, for Masonic purposes only.

Constituent Lodge

a Lodge chartered by, or under dispensation from, a Grand Lodge.

Constitution

Statuere meant that a thing was set, or placed, or established; when *con* was added *constituere* meant than an official ceremony had set, or fixed, or placed a thing. From the same source come statue, statute, institute, restitute, etc. A Lodge is "constituted" when it is formally and officially set up, and given its own permanent place in the Fraternity.

Contention

strife or struggle. Whenever and wherever men are grouped together for any purpose or a brotherhood is formed, differences of opinion will arise, conflicting interests will present themselves and the spirit of true brotherhood can be threatened. Among Freemasons, every effort must be put forth to prevent such circumstances from producing contention. Masons can agree to disagree.

Corinthian

one of the three classical (Greek) orders of architecture - the most ornamented of the three. Originated in the city of Corinth in Greece.

Cornerstone

this is usually the stone that lies at the corner of two walls of building in which certain historic documents are placed and on which historic inscriptions are engraved. In Masonic buildings, it is always placed at the northeast corner, and this position is preferred in buildings for which Masons perform the cornerstone-laying ceremony. Beautiful and meaningful symbolisms are associated with the laying of cornerstones as a dedication to the one living Great Architect of the Universe.

Covenant of Masons

A covenant is a contract or agreement between two or more parties on certain terms. In becoming a Mason, a man enters into a covenant with the Fraternity, agreeing to fulfill certain promises and perform certain duties. On the other hand, the Fraternity and its members bind themselves to certain ties of friendship, brotherliness, protection, support and benefits. The breaking of a covenant is subject to stated penalties.

Covering of a Lodge

The covering of a Lodge is no less than a clouded canopy, or starry-decked heaven, where all good Masons hope at last to arrive, by the aid of that theological ladder which Jacob in his vision saw ascending from earth to heaven; the three principal rounds of which are denominated Faith, Hope and Charity, and which admonish us to have faith in God, hope in immortality, and charity to all mankind. The greatest of these is charity; for our faith will be lost in sight; hope ends in fruition; but charity extends beyond the grave, through the boundless realms of eternity.

Cowan

the origin is unknown, but it may be early Scotch. A Masonic term which means intruder or one who accidentally enters where he is not wanted. This is not to be confused with the word eavesdropper or one who deliberately tries to overhear and see what is not meant for his eyes and ears.

Craft

In Anglo-Saxon, craft meant cunning, skill, power, dexterity, etc. The word became applied to trades and occupations calling for trained skill on the part of those practicing it. The distinction between such trades and those not requiring trained workmen, so rigidly maintained, was one of the hallmarks of the Middle Ages. Freemasonry is called a Craft, partly for historical reasons, partly because, unlike so many fraternities, it requires a training (given in the form of initiation ceremonies) of those seeking its membership.

Craftsmen

The term "craft" applies to persons collectively engaged in a trade or mechanical operation. It is used of operative Masons and the vast number of men employed in the building of the Temple are referred to as Craftsmen. In speculative Masonry, the entire Fraternity is spoken of as the Craft, whereas individual members are Craftsmen.

Cubit

an ancient unit of linear measure, originally equal to the length of the forearm from the tip of the middle finger to the elbow, or about 17 to 22 inches (43 to 56 centimeters). The sacred cubit is 36 inches; the profane cubit is 18 inches.

D

Darkness to Light

Physical darkness is symbolic of ignorance and of spiritual blindness. Applicants for the enlightenment of Freemasonry are, of course, in total ignorance of the rituals, teachings and symbols of the Order. They are, hence, required to enter the Lodge in complete darkness, symbolic of that ignorance. They are in search of Light, and this is given to them as they advance through the several Degrees of Masonry.

Dark

A lodge which closes for a time or permanently is said to be or have gone dark.

David

David was the youngest son of Jesse of Bethlehem who was chosen and anointed to become the successor of Saul as King of Israel while only a lad and shepherd of his father's flocks. He served King Saul as a musician, later as a military leader of some genius, bravery, and great heroism. However, he was bitterly persecuted by the King because of his jealousies. At the age of thirty, David was anointed King at Hebron and later established his throne at Jerusalem. He reigned forty years and was permitted by God to make extensive preparations for the building of the Temple which was later erected by his son and successor, Solomon. He was forbidden to build the Temple because he was a warrior while his son, Solomon, would be a man of peace.

Day

From the beginning, the period of twenty-four hours embracing one phase of light and one of darkness has been regarded as a day. Among the ancients, the day began at sunset and ended at sunset the next day instead of running from midnight to midnight.

Deacons

despite the fact that the bloom has been rubbed off by our slang use of it, this may be one of the most beautiful words in our language. In Greek, *diakonos* was a servant, a messenger, a waiting man. In the early Christian Church a deacon served at the Lord's Supper and administered alms to the poor; and the word still most frequently refers to such a church officer. It appears that the two Lodge offices of Senior and Junior Deacon were patterned on the church offices. Their duties comprehend general surveillance over the Lodge, the introduction of visitors, and to serve as proxy for the Worshipful Master in certain circumstances.

Death

The Masonic idea of death is accompanied with no gloom, because it is represented as physical sleep for an unknown period of time, from which there will be an awakening of the body and a resurrection of a spiritual body capable and fitted for eternal life. From beginning to end, the rituals of Freemasonry teach and symbolize the doctrine of man's immortality and repudiate every grain of the doctrine of *annihilation* at death. In Masonic philosophy, death is the symbol of initiation completed, in which the resurrection of the body will be its final consummation.

Decalogue

the Ten Commandments.

Dedication

The Latin *dedicatus* was a participial form of *dedicare*, the latter having the meaning of declare, devote, proclaim - the root from which "diction" comes. To dedicate a building means by public ceremony to declare it built for some certain purpose. Dedication and consecration are closely allied in meaning, but the latter is more religious in its purposes.

Degree

The Latin *gradus* from which are derived grade, gradual, graduation, etc., meant a step, or set of steps, particularly of a stair; when united with the prefix, *da*, meaning "down," it became degradus, and referred to steps, degrees, progress by marked stages. From this came our "degree," which is a step, or grade, in the progress of a candidate toward the consummation of his membership. Our habit of picturing the degrees as proceeding from lower to higher, like climbing a stair, is thus very close to the ancient and original meaning of the word.

Deputation

a group of words such as compute, repute, depute sprang from the Latin *putare*, which meant (among other things) to estimate, to think, to count among. From this came *deputatus*, to select, to appoint. The idea was that from a number of persons one was selected for a special duty, hence our word "deputy." A deputation is an instrument appointing some man or group of men to act for others officially. Our Deputy Grand Master is thus set apart to act in the place of the Grand Master on need, and a District Deputy Grand Master is so called because he is appointed by the Grand Master to act as his personal representative in a District.

Demit

(also spelled "dimit.") as a verb this hails from the Latin *dimettere*, to send away, to release, to let go; we have it in our "dismiss." To demit from an organization is, using the official form, to resign, to relinquish one's membership. It has this meaning in Masonry.

Destruction of the Temple

The Temple built by Solomon underwent many defamations and was several times stripped of its golden adornments and treasures, sometimes by foreign attacks and sometimes by Judean kings for payments of tribute. These were judgments sent upon the nation for apostasies. The final destruction of the Temple was the burden of many prophecies and took place as predicted by God under the onslaughts of the armies of Nebuchadnezzar (586 B.C.).

Dew of Hermon

The dews of Mount Hermon, and of Palestine in general, were sources of irrigation, fertilization and refreshment for vegetation and agricultural growth. The phrase is employed as a symbolic expression of the bedewing influences of Divine Grace.

Discalceation

while this is not as familiar to Masons as the preceding words, it should come into more popular use because it is the technical name to describe an important element in the ceremony of initiation. *Calceare* was the Latin for shoe, *calceatus* meant shod. When united with the prefix *dis*, meaning apart, or asunder, our discalceate was originated, the obvious meaning of which is the removal of one's shoes, as suggested in the familiar Bible passage, "Put off thy shoes from off thy feet, for the place whereon thou standest is holy ground." The ceremonial removal of the shoes is properly called the "rite of discalceation."

Dispensation

Pendere was the Latin word for a weight, the root from which came many English words, notably pendent, expend, spend, dispense, etc. With the prefix *dis*, explained in the preceding paragraph, dispendere meant to weigh out, to pay off, to expend. From this came dispensatus, meaning to manage, to regulate, to distribute. In our usage a dispensation is a written instrument by which authority is made over to a group of brethren to form a Lodge.

Distressed Worthy Brother

to go to the aid of a distressed worthy Brother is not only the duty of every Mason, but is solemnly enjoined by Holy Writ. Masons believe and practice the Bible's edict of "we are our Brother's keeper."

Divested

to deprive or take away from; to undress or remove clothing, ornaments or equipment.

Doors Shall Be Shut

The expression, "The doors shall be shut in the street when the sound of the grinding is low" refers to the decrepitude of old age.

Doric

one of the three classical (Greek) orders of architecture - the oldest and simplest of the three, originated in an area of ancient Greece known as Doris.

Dotage

An old man in his dotage is one who has suffered the loss of judgment and memory, and is in that state of intellectual decrepitude which makes him incapable of comprehending the lessons of Freemasonry. While it is not a very beautiful word, it is interesting. It first came into existence among the early English, Dutch, German, and Scandinavian peoples, generally in the form *dotten*, *dutten*, meaning to nod with drowsiness, to nap. Since it was old people who most frequently sat nodding in their chairs it became associated with old age. "An old man in his dotage" is one who nods or prattles like a sleepy child, and whose faculties have begun to decay through old age. Old age is never a bar to Masonic membership unless it has reached this stage.

Due

proper; according to accepted standards or procedures

Dues

In Latin *debere* meant to owe something; it is preserved in our familiar, too familiar, "debt," in debit, indebted, debenture, duty, dues, etc. Related is the French *devoir*, often employed in English, meaning a piece of work one is under obligation to do. The same idea appears in "duty," which means that which is due, or that which is owed, in the moral sense. Dues represent one's fixed and regular indebtedness to his Lodge which he placed himself under obligation to pay when he signed the by-laws.

Dust to Dust (or Dust To Earth)

Man's body was made from the earth and must return to dust in one form or another. The use of this phrase points to the mortality and frailty of the physical being and to the need of recognizing the immortality of the spirit of man.

E

Eavesdropper

Early European peoples used a word in various forms - *evese*, *obasa*, *opa*, etc., - which meant the rim, or edge, of something, like the edge of a field; it came in time to be applied wholly to the gutter which runs along the edge of a roof. (Our "over" comes from this root.) "Dropper" had an origin among the same languages, and meant that which drips, or dribbles, like water dropping from a thawing icicle. Eavesdrop, therefore, was the water which dripped from the eaves. If a man set himself to listen through a window or keyhole to what was going on in a house he had to stand so close that the eavesdropping would fall upon him, for which reason all prying persons, seeking by secret means what they have no business to know, came to be called eaves-droppers.

Edict

a decree or proclamation issued by an authority and having the force of law. The root of this word is the Latin *dicere*, speak; united with the prefix *e*, meaning out, to come forth, it produced *edicere*, meaning to proclaim, to speak out with authority. It came in time to be applied to the legal pronouncements of a sovereign or ruler speaking in his own name and out of his own authority. When a Grand Master issues a certain official proclamation in his own name and out of the authority vested in his office, it is an edict.

Edifice

a building, especially one of imposing appearance or size.

Emblem

This beautiful and significant word, so familiar to Masons, has historical affiliations with the original idea embodied in "mosaic work," on which something is said below. Emblem is derived from the Greek prefix *en*, meaning in, united with *ballein*, meaning cast, put. The word became applied to raised decorations on pottery, to inlay work, tessellated and mosaic work; and since such designs were nearly always formal and symbolical in character, emblem came to mean an idea expressed by a picture or design. As Bacon put it, an emblem represents an intellectual conception in a sensible image. It belongs to that family of words of which type, symbol, figure, allegory, and metaphor are familiar members.

Emblem of Innocence

Throughout the Holy Scriptures, the lamb is used as an emblem of innocence, and the white leather lambskin apron is regarded as an emblem of purity after which Masons ever strive for in life.

Engrave

to cut figures or letters into wood, metal or other material

Ephraimites

members of one of the twelve tribes of Israel, descended from Ephraim, one of the sons of Jacob

Esoteric

this word is the opposite of exoteric. The root of it is the Greek *eso*, within. It means that which is secret, in the inner circle. Exoteric is that which is outside. In Masonry the "esoteric work" is that part of the Ritual, which it is illegal to publish, while the exoteric is that part which, is published in the Monitor.

Etch

to produce as a pattern on a hard service by eating into the material's surface as with acid or any means of shallow scratches

Equivocation

the use of equivocal language, e.g., words capable of two interpretations, cryptic, evasive, ambiguous - to avoid committing oneself to what one says; uncertainty; uncertain or questioning disposition or mind

Eternal Life

The immortality of the soul is a fundamental dogma of Freemasonry. Hence, the faith and belief in eternal life beyond the grave. The doctrine of a future resurrection of the body is also a tenet of Freemasonry.

Evergreen

having foliage that persists and remains green throughout the year. In Masonry, the evergreen is used as a symbol of the immortality of the soul.

F

Faithful Servant

The faithful servant is one who is diligent in his stewardship, dutiful to his master and loyal in the face of temptation and trial.

Fatherhood of God

Masonry believes that man is the offspring of God by creation, that God made mankind all of one blood and that God is, by virtue of His creation of man and of His goodness to man, man's Father.

Fellow

In Anglo Saxon, *lagu* (from which we have "law") meant that which was permanently ordered, fixed, set; *fe* meant property; *fela* suggested properties set together, in other words, a partnership. From this we have "fellow," a companion, mate, partner, an equal, a peer. A man became a "fellow" in a Medieval guild or corporation when admitted a member on the same terms as all others, sharing equally in the duties, rights, and privileges. In Operative Masonry, in order to be a fellow a man had to be a Master Mason, in the sense of having passed through his apprenticeship, so that Masters were fellows and fellows were

Masters. Prior to about 1740 "Fellow of the Craft" and "Master Mason" referred to the same grade or degree, but at about that year a new division in ranking was made, and "Fellow Craft" was the name given to the Second Degree in the new system, "Master Mason" to the Third.

Fiat

an authoritative decree, sanction or order; a command or act of will that creates something without, or as if without, further effort; an arbitrary decree or order.

Fiat Lux

Latin for: *Let There be light*

Flight to Joppa

The story of Jonah's flight to Joppa in his effort to escape a Divinely-entrusted responsibility and service for God is strikingly used in Masonic ritual.

Foreign Country

This expression, which is employed of the travels of Master Masons of the operative class following the completion of the Temple in search of labor and for wages, is correctly understood by few who hear it. In its symbolic meaning, it does not refer to the activities of those who have completed the Master Degree. Hence, Heaven is the "foreign country" into which Master Masons travel, where the True Word, not given in this life, is to be received, and where the Master Mason is to receive his wages.

Form

We speak of the "form of the Lodge," "due form," etc. The

word is derived from the Latin *forma*, which meant the shape, or figure, or frame of anything; also it was used of a bench, or seat, whence the old custom of calling school benches "forms." It is the root of formal, formation, informal, and scores of other English words equally familiar. The "form of the Lodge" is its symbolical shape; a ceremony is in "due form" if it has the officially required character or framework of words and actions.

Fortitude

The key to the meaning of this magnificent word lies in its derivation from the Latin *fords*, meaning strong, powerful, used in the Middle Ages of a stronghold, or fort. Force, enforce, fortify, fortification, forceful, are from the same root. A man of fortitude has a character built strong like a fort, which can be neither taken by bribe nor over-thrown by assault, however strong may be the enemy, or however great may be the suffering or deprivation within. One is reminded of Luther's great hymn, "A mighty fortress is our God." The importance and essential value of this virtue of true manhood for Masons is enforced by the use of the story of unfaltering courage and faith of the three Hebrew children in the fiery furnace and by Daniel's bravery in the lion's den.

Foundation

The deeply laid and solid foundation of the Temple strikingly symbolizes the necessity for a good foundation in the building of character and in life's vocations.

Forty-Seventh Problem of Euclid

The forty-seventh problem of Euclid's first book, which has been adopted as a symbol in the Master's Degree, is thus enunciated: "In any right-angled triangle, the square which is described upon the side subtending the right angle is equal to the squares described upon the sides which contain the right angle." Thus, in a triangle whose perpendicular is 3 feet, the square of which is 9, and whose base is 4 feet, the wquare of which is 16, the hypotenuse, or subtending side, will be 5 feet, the square of which will be 25, which is the sum of 9 and 16. This interesting problem, on account of its great utility in making calculations and drawing plans for buildings, is sometimes called the "Carpenter's Theorum."

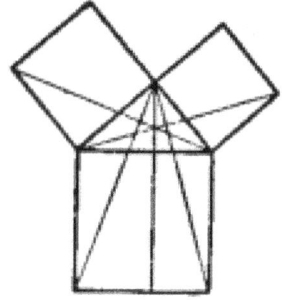

This was an invention of our ancient friend and brother, the great Pythagoras, who, in his travels through Asia, Africa, and Europe, was initiated into several orders of Priesthood, and raised to the sublime degree of Master Mason. This wise philosopher enriched his mind abundantly in a general knowledge of things and more especially in Geometry, or Masonry. On this subject he drew out many problems and theorems; and among the most distinguished, he erected this, which, in the joy of his heart, he call Eureka, in the Grecian language signifying, I have found it; and upon the discovery of which he is said to have sacrificed a hecatomb. It teaches Masons to be general lovers of the arts and sciences.

Fraternal Intercourse

activities that promote fraternalism in constituent Lodges. This is normally held to be the exchange of words, signs and grips that are reserved for known Masons.

Fraternity

This the most prized, perhaps, of all words in Masonry, harks back to the Latin *frater*, which is so closely allied to "brother," as already noted in the section on that word. It gives us *fra, frater, fraternize,* and many other terms of the same import. A fraternity is a society in which the members strive to live in a brotherly concord patterned on the family relations of blood brothers, where they are worthy of the tie. To be fraternal means to treat another man as if he were a brother in the most literal sense.

Free

The origin of the use of the term "free" in speculative Masonry is in the fact that the operative Masons who worked on King Solomon's Temple were exempted from imposts, duties and taxes as were their descendants. They were, therefore, declared to be "free."

G

"G"

The letter "G" is one of the most sacred symbols in Freemasonry. It has a double meaning, representing, first, the Supreme Deity as the Great Architect of the Universe and the one true and living God of all Masons; and, secondly, the preeminence of the science of geometry in the rituals of Freemasonry. In this twofold symbolism, the letter "G" represents to the Mason unity of Heaven with the earth, of the Divine Being with the human, of the temporal with the eternal, and of the finite with the infinite.

Gage

Gage (also spelled "gauge") has an uncertain ancestry. Early French and English
peoples had *gauger, gagen*, etc., which referred
to the measuring of wine casks; some believe
our "gallon" and "gill" to have been thus derived. Its meaning became enlarged to include
any kind of measuring, literally or figura-
tively. The instrument used to do the measuring came to be called "the gage." Among Op-
erative Masons it was used to measure a stone for cutting to the
required "twenty-four-inch gage" is such a measuring rod or
stick marked off into twenty-four inches.

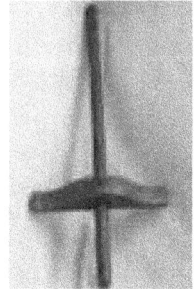

Gates of the Temple

The Temple of Solomon had only one entrance or portal,
but the walls of the enclosure had a gate at each points of the
compass. Freemasonry makes special symbolic use of three of
these gates, the one on the east, the one on the west, and the one
on the south. These gates are symbols of the progress of the sun,
rising in the east, reaching its zenith in the south, and setting in
the west. They also symbolize birth, life, and death as well as
youth, manhood and old age.

Geometry

It is unfortunate that for
most schoolroom drudgery has
robbed this beautiful word of its
poetry. The Greek *geo* (in compounds) was earth, land; *metron*
was measure. The original ge-
ometer was a landmeasurer, a
surveyor, but his methods be-

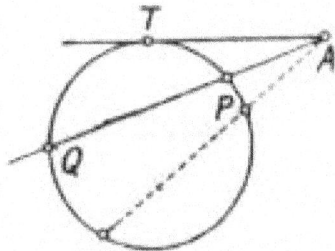

came broadened and applied to many other kinds of problems, so that at last his craft became a portion of the art of mathematics. Geometry, that branch of mathematics which deals with figures in space, is associated in every Mason's mind with the immortal Euclid, who figures 50 prominently in all the ancient Masonic manuscripts. It achieved its great place in Freemasonry because of its constant and prime importance in the builders' art. Symbolically speaking geometry (to it the Letter G originally referred), consists of all those fixed principles and laws of morality and of thought to which a right character and a true mind adjust themselves.

Good Standing, In

when dues are current and one is an Active Member of the lodge or when one is defined as such by the lodge or Grand Lodge laws

Grammar

The Greeks had *graphein*, to write, or draw (from this we have graphic, engrave, etc.) ; gramma was that which was written or drawn. Grammar now refers only to the skeletonal framework of language, its parts of speech and their combinations, but formerly it included all forms of learning based on language, such as rhetoric and what is now taught in the schools as English; by the time our Monitors were written, however, grammar and rhetoric had become differentiated. In interpreting the Second Degree this wide meaning of "grammar" must be kept in mind.

Grand

Grandis in the Latin meant great, large, awesome, especially in the sense of imposing; it was afterwards applied to the aged, the ripe in experience, an application easy enough to understand when one recalls the reverence paid by the Romans to seniority, long experience, etc. this latter meaning appears in our grandfather, grandmother, grandsire, etc. In English the word developed in two directions, one toward that which is great, large, awe-in-spiring, as in "grandeur," the other toward dignity, exalted power. Our own use of the term in "Grand" Lodge, "Grand" East, "Grand" Master, harks back to the latter of the two usages. The head of the Craft is called "Grand"' Master because he is its most exalted official.

Grasshopper Shall Be A Burden

symbolic of the weakness accompanying old age.

Great Porch

this was the name give to the vestibule at the entrance into the Temple of Solomon.

Great and Sacred Name

Any name that is used as a title of Deity is held sacred by Freemasons, and all names of our God are to be uttered with profound reverence and never thoughtlessly or blasphemously.

Great White Throne

this term refers to the pure and glorious throne of God. Before it, every knee must bow to the Glory of the Father.

Grip

Grip, grope, grab, grasp, gripe came the same roots. The Anglo Saxon *gripe* meant to clutch, to lay hold of, to seize, to grasp strongly. A grip means

to clasp another's hand firmly; it differs from a mere handclasp, which may be a meaningless formality, in that it is done earnestly, and for a purpose—for what purpose in our fraternal system every Mason knows. A grip should be given as if one meant it; half of its meaning lies in the way it is done.

Ground Floor of the Lodge

Mount Moriah, the site on which Solomon's Temple was erected, is symbolically referred to as the "ground floor of the Lodge."

Guttural

from the Latin *guttur*, the throat, or having to do with, or involving the throat

H

Harodim

the title given to the overseers and princes appointed by Solomon to supervise the workmen preparing the material and in the building of the Temple.

Hecatomb

a sacrifice to the ancient Greek and Roman gods consisting originally of 100 oxen or cattle.

Healing

Healing is a process used in some jurisdictions to accept a Mason from an irregular lodge into a regular lodge. The process may be but an administrative procedure or may be one of retaking some or all of the craft degrees or obligations.

Heaven

A distinctive tenet of Freemasonry is that there is a Heaven of bliss beyond the grave. The symbolic meaning of the "foreign country" in which the Master Mason seeks wages is Heaven, the higher state of man's existence after death and following the Resurrection.

Hele, Hale

to hide or conceal; to cover; to keep out of view.

Heredom

The most plausible understanding of "Heredom" was given in 1858, by a writer in the London Freemasons Magazine. He traces it to the two Greek words, *repass hieros*, meaning holy, and *biros domos*, meaning house. It would thus refer to Freemasonry as symbolically the Holy House or Temple. In this way the title of Rose Croix of Heredom would signify the Rosy Cross of the Holy House of Freemasonry. This derivation is now very generally recognized as the true one.

High Twelve

The Latin *nonus* referred to the ninth hour of the day, that is, nine hours after sunrise. In the Medieval church it referred to the middle hour between midday and sunset, that is, about three o'clock P.M. In the course of time it came to refer to any part of the middle of the day, and finally to twelve o'clock. The origin of our "High Twelve" is uncertain, but it is probable that it goes back to a time before "noon" was generally used for twelve o'clock; the "high" doubtless refers to the sun, which at that time was at its highest point in the sky.

Hills and Valleys

In ancient times, and even today, high elevations suggest the worship of God. The hilltop or mountaintop is a symbol of "Holiness unto the Lord."

Hiram

The gavel, when wielded by the Master of the Lodge, is sometimes called the Hiram, because as the workmen at the Temple were controlled and directed by Hiram, the chief builder, so the Master keeps order in the Lodge by proper use of the gavel.

Hiram Abif

see: *Abif*

Homage

special honor or respect shown or expressed publicly.

Hoodwink

"Hood" goes back to old German and Anglo Saxon, in which it referred to head covering, as in hat, hood, helmet, etc.; "wink," in the same languages, meant to close the eyes, "wench," "wince," etc., being similarly derived. A hoodwink was therefore a headdress designed to cover the eyes. The popular use of the word is believed to go back to the old sport of falconry, once so popular, in which the falcon had a hood over its eyes until ready to strike at its prey.

Holiness

Throughout Masonic ritual, the absolute and superlative Holiness of God is recognized, and every representation of the

Deity in symbols, attitudes and words must be in the most reverent manner.

Holy of Holies

The ancient Tabernacle erected by Moses at Mount Sinai was divided into two compartments or rooms. At the west end was the Most Holy Place constructed of a perfect cube fifteen feet in all dimensions. It was separated from the other room, the Holy Place, by curtains. The only article of furniture in the Holy of Holies was the Ark of the Covenant which contained the Book of Law, the stone tablets on which God had written the Ten Commandments, a pot of manna and Aaron's rod that budded. The Most Holy Place was entered only by a high priest once each year on the Great Day of Atonement. Like the Tabernacle, King Solomon's Temple was divided into two compartments. The Most Holy Place was a perfect cube forty feet in all its dimensions. All the walls were overlaid with fine gold as was the floor.

Holy Place

One of the two compartments of the Tabernacle of Moses was the Holy Place or Sanctuary at the east end of the Tabernacle. The furniture of the Holy Place consisted of the great Candlestick, the table for shewbread and the altar of incense with its censer and snuffers. In King Solomon's Temple, the Holy Place, sometimes referred to as the Greater House, followed the pattern of the Tabernacle, but was much larger. Instead of one candlestick, there were ten: five on the right side and five on the left, all made of pure gold. The Altar of Incense occupied the west end of the Sanctuary and was also made of pure gold, as was it censer.

Hour Glass, The

is an emblem of human life. "Behold how swiftly the sands run, and how rapidly our lives are drawing to a close!"

House

This term is used to mean any of the various Masonic bodies. A "Blue House" would be a craft lodge.

House Not Made With Hands

This expression comprehends the eternal dwelling place of God and the resurrected and glorified body of the redeemed in the life beyond.

Human Senses

There is here the recognition of the truth that all the natural faculties and endowments of man are the products of the creative energy of God and are loving gifts from Him.

I

I Am That I Am

This is the English translation of the most distinctive and significant title of Jehovah God given to Moses at the burning bush. In its original Hebrew form, it was regarded with such sacredness by the Israelites that it was never spoken above a whisper. It signifies the "self-existent, independent, unsearchable One."

Immemorial

Reaching beyond the limits of memory, tradition, or recorded history.

Immortality

Much of the ritual in Freemasonry assumes the doctrine of man's immortality, and in many specific instances, professions of this fundamental tenet are uttered.

Impart

to give; to communicate knowledge of something; to make known; tell; relate

Indite

to write down; to put down in writing

Indwelling of God

That God deigns to dwell among his people and with the hearts of the pure and the good is a fundamental truth to Masons.

Ineffable Name

It is generally agreed among the Believers that the correct pronunciation of the most sacred name of God has been lost, and to this traditional fact Masons assent. In it believed, however, that the mysteries of this Ineffable Name is held by the Messiah until the Day of Resurrection.

Initiation

The Latin *initium* means beginning, as in our initial"; *initiatus*, the participle from the verb *initiare*, referred to any act incident to the beginning or introduction of a thing. The word came widely into use in mysteries and sacred rites, whence it has come into our Masonic nomenclature. Back of it, as used by us, is the picture of birth, so that the Masonic initiation means that a candidate has been born into the Masonic life, making the same kind of symbolic beginning therein that a babe makes when born into the world.

A Masonic initiation is a personal, meaningful experience where there has been a desire to initiate, a desire to be initiated and the proper, solemn setting for the initiation.

Injunction

an order or requirement placed upon someone by a superior

Inner Door

Just as the mysteries of God's truth are available to those who earnestly knock, so admittance to the lessons of Freemasonry are opened by the proper knock at the Inner Door of the Lodge.

Innocence

From time immemorial, the lamb has been regarded as an emblem of innocence. Since Masons are required to strive after perfect innocence, especially in the Masonic conduct, the apron worn by them must be made of pure white lambskin.

Installation

Stallum was the Late Latin for place, or seat, or proper position, which meaning is preserved in our English "stall." To "install" therefore means that one has been placed in his seat or station—the "in" meaning here the same as in English. A Masonic installation is a ceremony by which an elected officer is officially placed in the seat to which his brethren have elected him.

Interment

the act or ritual of interring or burying. The grave is the natural resting place for the bodies of the dead, but it is not the final abode of the spirit. We honor our dead in interment, but we await their Resurrection.

Invest

to give; to furnish; to clothe

Inviolate

not broken or disregarded; not told to others; respected Light knowledge or understanding

Ionic

one of the three classical (Greek) orders of architecture, originated in an area of ancient Greece known as Ionia

Iron Tools

In order that perfect quiet and reverence might prevail in the building of the Temple of Solomon, no iron tool of any kind was employed.

J

Jachin

The two great pillars of Solomon's Temple supporting the Great Porch, known as Solomon's Porch, were
called Boaz and Jachin. Jachin is a combination of two
words, *Jah*, the poetical name of Jehovah, and *iachin*,
meaning establishment. The full significance of the name
is, therefore, "With God's help to establish," the symbolical meaning given to in the work of Freemasonry.

Jacob's Ladder

The story of Jacob's dream or vision is which he saw a stairway leading from earth to Heaven and angels descending and
ascending on it holds an important place in Masonic ritual. It is
employed as a symbol of the progressive course from earth to
Heaven, and of the transition from death to life.

Jah

the poetical name of Jehovah.

Japhet

the eldest son of Noah. It is said that the first ark — the Ark
of Safety, the archetype of the Tabernacle — was constructed by
Shem, Ham, and Japhet under the superintendence of Noah.
Hence these are significant words to the Royal Arch Mason.

Jesus and the Temple

Jesus was carried to the Temple when he was only forty days old for purification ceremonies. Again at twelve, for Passover in Jerusalem and later for public ministry.

Judah

Judah, the fourth son of Jacob and the founder of the tribe bearing his name, is also the representative of a key point in ancient Masonry. Judah distinguished himself on a number of occasions and was given Messianic distinction in the tribal blessings of his father and by Moses. The royal house of Israel was of the tribe of Judah, even as was Jesus. The tribe of Judah was the first to cross the Jordan and enter the Promised Land. For this reason, and because of its distinction as the tribe of David, Solomon and Jesus, Judah represents or symbolizes the entrance of the candidate into the Light and liberty of Freemasonry.

Judicious

having, exercising or characterized by sound judgement; discrete; wise

Junior Past Master

a Mason who served as Master of a lodge the year before.

Junior Warden

The "Third in Command" of a lodge. Similar to "Second Vice-President" in other organizations.

K

Kadosh

In the AASR, this is the 30th degree. The word is Hebrew, and signifies holy or consecrated, and is thus intended to denote the elevated character of the Degree and the sublimity of the truths which distinguish it and its possessors from the other Degrees. The Degree of Kadosh, though found in many of the Rites and in various countries, seems, in all of them, to have been more or less connected with the Knights Templar.

Keepers of the House Shall Tremble

This expression is a figure of the failings of the body in old age or as weakened by the approach of death. The usual interpretation is that the arms and legs are the keepers.

Keystone

The stone placed in the center of an arch which preserves the others in their places, and secures firmness and stability to the arch. As it was formerly the custom of Operative Masons to place a peculiar mark on each stone of a building to designate the workman by whom it had been adjusted, so the Keystone was most likely to receive the most prominent mark, that of the Superintendent of the structure.

Kilwinning

As the city of York claims to be the birthplace of Freemasonry in England, the obscure little village of Kilwinning is entitled to the same honor with respect to the origin of Freemasonry in Scotland.

L

Labor

The Latin *labor* meant toil, work, the putting forth of effort; it appears to be akin to *robur,* or strength, preserved in our "robust." While labor and work are used interchangeably, the latter is a more generic word, and admits of a much wider range of uses. Work may be either hard or easy but labor is always hard; work is used of all sorts of effort; labor refers generally to muscular effort, followed by fatigue. When labor is kept up unremittingly it is toil; and when toil is uninteresting, uninspiring, and poorly paid it is drudgery. When working, one's ambition is to succeed with it; when laboring, one looks forward to resting from it; hence, it is from labor that we seek refreshment, not from work.

Landmark

In ancient times, it was customary to mark the boundaries of lands by the means of stone pillars or heaps of stones. The removal of such landmarks was a grievous crime and an evidence of fraudulent intent by the offender. In speculative Masonry there are also landmarks, and the same rigid rule with reference to ancient landmarks applies to these. The landmarks of Masonry are those principles by which the Craft is bounded, that is, marked off from all other societies and associations and without which it would lose its identity.

Lay or Inlay

The manner or position in which something is situated (lay). To set (a piece of wood, metal, etc.) into a surface to form a design that is usually level with the surface (inlay).

Legend

The Greeks had *legein*, speak; the Latins *legere*, read; from these we have legend, lecture, etc. In the early Christian church the legend was the Scripture selection read in a church service; later the term became applied to stories about the lives of the saints, especially to their wonders and miracles. The famous "Golden Legend," a collection of such stories, was one of the most popular books of the Middle Ages. Legend, as now used, is a story without historical foundations but told in the form of history, hence our "Legend of the Third Degree," a narrative in dramatic form that Masons have long understood to be non-historical.

Level of Equality

The level in Masonry is a symbol of the fraternal equality of mankind as the offspring of God, all races and nations having been made of one blood. The fundamental principle that all men are created equal, with certain inalienable rights to life, liberty and the pursuit of happiness is basic in Freemasonry. We meet upon the "level" because Masonic rights, duties, and privileges are the same for all members without distinction.

Lewis

A candidate for the Degrees of Masonry whose father is a Master Mason. In the same sense, the French use *louveteau*.

The operative tool known as the *lewis* was an iron clamp capable of exerting outward pressure when inserted in a cavity in the top of a stone. By that means, a stone could be raised and put in place with no chains or clamps on the outside to interfere with the setting of it. The clamp was then released and the lewis withdrawn. The

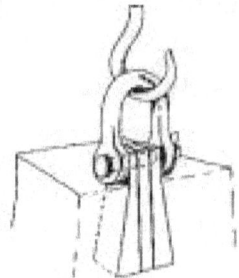

transferal of this term to symbolic use has been the subject of some speculation. It is said that as the lewis is used to assist in the lifting of stones, so the Lewis assists and supports the father. The term appears in the English Constitutions of 1738 near the close of the Deputy Grand Master's song.

Libertine

Liber was the Latin for "free," as in our liberty, liberal, etc. When the Romans gave a slave his freedom he was called *libertus*, so that in Roman history a libertine was a freedman. In theology a libertine came to mean one who holds loose views in regard to morality, a immoral person who flouts moral laws. The early Freemasons employed the later use of the word.

Light

Throughout the ritual and work of Freemasonry, Light is the symbol of knowledge, and just as God spoke into existence physical light, so He is the original source of all true knowledge. The Great Light of Masonry is His inspired work. Masons are pledged to strive after more and more Light as life goes on and should seek above all things Light Eternal. By an inevitable association the word came into metaphorical use to mean the coming of truth and knowledge into the mind. When a candidate ceases to be ignorant of Masonry, when through initiation the truths of Masonry have found entrance into his mind, he is said to be "enlightened" in the Masonic sense.

Light of Life

The source of enlightenment and knowledge for life's darkness, perplexities and doubts, as well as for life's responsibilities and duties, is the Holy Bible — the Great Light of Masonry.

Lily Work

The lily is an emblem of peace and purity. For this reason, lily work occupied a place of conspicuousness and distinction in the ornamentations of the Temple and its furniture.

Lion of the Tribe of Judah

In the tribal benediction pronounced upon Judah, the "lion's whelp" is used emblematically of strength. Hence, the ensign on the banner of Judah was a lion. The phrase in the Masonic ritual, "The lion of the tribe of Judah," is Messianic and refers to Christ.

Lodge

This word comes from the Old French, English and Medieval Latin, and meant generally a hut, a cottage, a gallery, a covered way, etc.; our "lobby" had the same beginning. How the Operative Masons came to employ the term, and just what they meant by it, has never been determined; they had a symbolic Lodge, their building was a Lodge, the group of members was a Lodge, an assembly of Masons was a Lodge, and often times the whole body of Masons was called a Lodge. In our own usage the word has three technical meanings; the place where Masons meet, the assembly of the brethren duly congregated for labor, and a piece of furniture.

Lost Word

The lost word was the ineffable name of God, but the term is used symbolically of Divine Truth.

M

Manual

relating to the hand, from the Latin *manus*, a hand.

Mason

This is a word from the Middle Ages, with an uncertain origin. The old Gothic *maitan* meant to hew, or cut, and it is supposed the word carried that general meaning through Medieval Latin, English, German, and in the Scandinavian languages. If at first it was used only of a stone-cutter, it came later to mean a builder. Why the Operatives were called "Freemasons" is still an unsolved puzzle; the most likely view is that they were a society of builders free to move from one place to another in contrast to the gild Masons who were confined in their labors to one community. In our Fraternity a Mason is a builder of manhood and brotherhood.

Masonic age

the symbolic *Masonic age* corresponds to the different degrees obtained by the Mason. For a Master Mason, his Masonic age is three.

Masonic regalia

aprons, jewels, implements and hats appropriate to one's station or office.

Master

The Latin root *mag* had the general meaning of great—as in "magnitude"; it was the source of the Latin magister, head, chief, principal, the word of which "magistrate" was made. During the Middle Ages it fell into use as a conventional title applied to persons in superior rank, preserved in our own familiar "mister," always written "Mr," a colloquial form of "master." Also it came to be used of a man who had overcome the difficulties in learning an art, thereby proving himself to be greater than his task, as when it is said of an artist who has overcome all the obstacles and difficulties of painting, "He is a master." A Master Mason is so called because be has proved himself capable of mastering the work; also because he belongs to a Degree so named.

Master of the Lodge

This title signifies "teacher," not Lord. The Master of the Lodge should be well informed in the mysteries, symbols, allegories and principles of Freemasonry. Masonry is a science of morals, clothed in symbols and any Brother who becomes a teacher of this science must fully understand the allegories in which it is enveloped, the symbolisms with which it is illustrated, the myths and legends of Masonry, and their mystical applications to everyday life. What the sun is by day to the world, the Master is to the Lodge.

Master Builder

In the material realm, a master builder is one who is qualified in intellect and training to do constructive building of symmetrical and perfect order — an architect, skilled worker and capable artisan. Hiram Abif, the widow's son of the tribe of Naphtali, was such a master builder. With the very best materials furnished him by King Solomon, he carried to completion an edifice of magnificence and superlative beauty and glory. In speculative Masonry, a master builder is one who is qualified in heart and mind, by skill in moral and spiritual science, and by Holy consecration to erect temples of immortal characters.

Mercenary

motivated solely by a desire for monetary or material gain.

Metal Tools

In ancient Israel, the use of metal tools in the actual construction of sacred altars and edifices was forbidden; hence, the preparation of all materials for the building of Solomon's Temple was done in the forests and quarries.

Money Changers

These were exchange bankers who set up tables in the precincts of the Temple where they provided Jewish coins for Temple offerings in exchange for foreign moneys, charging fees for their services. Jesus drove them from the Temple, declaring that they had made the "House of Prayer a den of thieves."

Monitor

The Latin *monere* meant to warn; it was the root of our admonish, admonition, etc.; a monitor was the man who did the warning. The term became widely used in early school systems of the senior pupils in a class whose duty it was to instruct his juniors; from this it passed to include the book, the blackboard and other instruments used by him in his teachings. Our use of it carries this last meaning; the Masonic Monitor is a book for teaching a candidate the exoteric work.

Mosaic

This word has nothing to do with Moses. Its root was the Greek *mousa*, a muse, suggesting something artistic. The same root appears in our "museum," literally a place where artistic work is exhibited. Through the Latin it came into modern languages and during the Middle Ages became narrowed down to mean a pattern formed by small pieces of inlay, a form of decorative work much in vogue during the time of the Operative Masons. Our mosaic pavement is so called because it consists of an inlay pattern, small black and white squares alternating to suggest day and night.

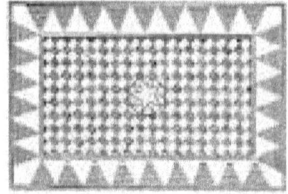

Mother Lodge

The lodge in which one is made a Mason. The first lodge to which a Mason joined, regardless of how many other lodges he joins.

Mouth to Ear

The Freemason is taught by an expressive symbol, to whisper good counsel in his Brother's ear, and to warn him of approaching danger. "It is a rare thing," says Bacon, "except it be from a perfect and entire friend, to have counsel given that is not bowed and crooked to some ends which he hath that giveth it." And hence it is an admirable lesson, which Freemasonry here teaches us, to use the lips and the tongue only in the service of a Brother.

Mystic Tie

This phrase refers to the bond of fraternal love, to the solemn vows of eternal Masonry, irrespective of differences in race, nationality and conflicting interests. By this mystic tie, men of the most discordant opinions are united in one band, meet at one altar, even when fighting in opposing armies or affiliated with different religions. It is, indeed, an indefinable spiritual tie, and those under its influence are rightly spoken of as "Brethrenof the Mystic Tie."

N

Names of the Temple

The Temple built by Solomon, which occupies such importance throughout the symbolisms and legends of Freemasonry, is given a number of names in the Bible: The Palace of Jehovah, The House of Sanctuary, and The House of Ages.

Naphtali

Naphtali was the fifth son of Jacob and the founder of the tribe bearing his name. In the tribal blessing given him by his father, and confirmed by Moses, wise counsel and prosperity were to be the chief characteristics of the tribe. Naphtali represents the investiture of the lambskin apron bestowed in the West and South.

Noah

In all the old Masonic manuscript Constitutions that are extant, Noah and the Flood play an important part in the Legend of the Craft. Hence, as the Masonic system became developed, the Patriareh was looked upon as what was called a Patron of Freemasonry.

North Side

In Masonic symbolism the North Side of the Lodge represents God's exalted throne.

Northeast Corner

As one progresses through the rites and symbolisms of Freemasonry, receiving more and more Light, he reaches the Northeast Corner with all the outward appearances of a perfect and upright Mason, a true and tried representative of the cornerstone of a great moral and spiritual edifice.

Notice

a call issued by the Secretary, by order of the Lodge or Master, or by other competent authority to attend or perform as specified. A notice is not the same as a *Summons*.

O

Obligation

From time immemorial, men have entered into covenants of brotherhood and friendship under solemn obligations of fidelity and loyalty, and whenever the circumstances and purposes warranted it, secrecy has been pledged. This practice among Masons has many precedents and is based on the truths and principles set forth of the Great Light of Masonry. All obligations voluntarily taken in Masonry must be faithfully performed and are never subject to revocation. The obligation is the tie, or bond, itself; in Masonry a formal and voluntary pledge on the candidate's part by virtue of which he is accepted as a responsible member of the family of Masons.

Oblong

This has long been a puzzle word in Masonic nomenclature. How, it is asked, can a square be oblong, when a square is equal on all its sides? The answer is that in this connection "square" is used in the sense of rectangle; the angles are squared, not the sides. Oblong is derived from *ob*, near, or before, and *longus*, long; that is, it means something approximately long, so that the main axis is much longer than the others, as a slender leaf, a shaft, etc. An "oblong square" is a rectangle of which two opposite sides are much longer than the other two. The Lodge symbolically is an oblong square in this sense.

Opening of the Lodge

It is absolutely necessary that the Lodge be opened in due and ancient form. Without these ceremonies, the assembly is not a Masonic Lodge. This is true because the Master must be reminded of the dignity and character of himself and of his position. And the other officers must be impressed with the respect and veneration due from their sundry stations. But more important, the Fraternity in Lodge assembly and in work must maintain a reverential awe for Deity, and must look to the Great Light of Freemasonry, the Holy Bible, for guidance and instruction. Thus, in the opening of the Lodge, the Great Architect of the Universe must be worshipped, and His blessings upon the work about to be performed must be supplicated. At the same time, prayer is offered for peace and harmony in the closing of the Lodge.

Operative

We distinguish Operative Masons, builders of the Middle Ages, founders of Masonry, from Spectulative Masons, present members of the Fraternity, using the builders' tools as emblems and symbols. The Latin for toil, or work, was *opus*, still used in that form in English to signify a musical or literary achievement. *Opus* was the root of *operari*, to work, whence we have our operate, operative, operation, opera, operator, and many others. The Operative Mason was one who toiled at building in the plain, literal sense of the word. "Speculative" will be explained farther in this publication.

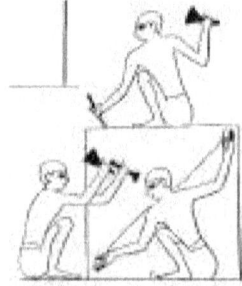

Ordo ab chao

Latin for: *Order from chaos*. This phrase is normally associated with the Scottish Rite.

Ornament

Ornare was the Latin verb meaning to adorn, to equip, of which the noun was *amamen* turn, trappings, embellishment, furniture, etc., from which was derived our "adornment" and "ornament." In church usage "ornaments" was the name given to all the equipment used in the services of divine worship. We speak of the mosaic pavement, the indented tessel, and blazing star as "ornaments of the Lodge;" whether the term was used by Lodges originally because they were considered to be adornments, or because they were part of the Lodge equipment it is impossible to say, though the latter alternative appears to be the more likely.

P

Passions

great emotion; the emotions as distinguished from reason; powerful or compelling feelings or desires.

Password

The Latin *passus* meant pace, step, track, passage; it contains the picture of a path, road, aisle, or door through which one can make his way, hence our "pass," derived from it. From it also we have our word "pace." A password is any agreed word or counter-sign that permits one to pass through an entrance or passage otherwise closed.

Peace on Earth

The principles and tenets of Freemasonry teach "peace on earth and good will to men."

Pearly Gates

The splendor and beauty and glory of Solomon's Temple and of its appointments were but symbols and prophecies of the superior Temple, that house not made with hands, eternal in the Heavens, with its gates of pearl.

Pectoral

belonging to the breast; from the Latin *pectus*, the breast.

Pedal

belonging to the feet, from the Latin *pedes*, the feet.

Penalty

It is significant that our "penal" derives from the Latin for pain, *paena*, the root of our penance, penalty, penitence, penitentiary, punish, primitive, pine, and a circle of similar English words. It has the meaning of pain inflicted for the purpose of correction, discipline, or protecting society, never the infliction of pain for its own sake. Our own penalties are symbolical in form, their language being derived from early English forms of punishment for heresy and treason.

Perfect Points of Entrance

symbolic action called for on entrance into a lodge. Every Mason has four perfect points of entrance which are beautifully illustrated in the four Cardinal Virtues: Temperance, Fortitude, Prudence, and Justice.

Pillar

The Latin *pila* was a pile,—such as a pile under a house—a pier, a pillar, or a mole,— the last named a massive stonework enclosing a harbor. In ancient times pillars were used for all manner of religious and symbolical purposes, as when Jacob erected a pillar at a grave, or Solomon set up two great pillars— the prototype of ours—on the Porch before his Temple.

Pillars of Brass

Important and significant features of the architecture of King Solomon's Temple were two giant bronze shafts which stood in striking relief in front of the entrance to the Great Porch at the east entrance of the Temple, one on the left and one on the right. Each was seventy feet high and twenty-four feet in circumference. They were highly ornamented by a network of brass overhung with wreaths of bronze pomegranates, each row containing one hundred. Each of these giant pillars had a chapiter at the top, ten feet in length, making the total height of each pillar eighty feet. On the top of these chapiters were great bowls for oil, called pommels, over which were hung festoon-like wreaths of pomegranates, interspersed at various points with lily work. These two great shafts were given the names Boaz and Jachin.

Pillars of Wisdom

The seven great pillars of wisdom are regarded by Masons to be of superlative worth in the building of a moral and spiritual edifice.

Pitcher Be Broken at the Fountain

The heart is the fountain of human life, and the great vein which carries the blood to the right ventricle is symbolically called the pitcher. When this is broken as a result of the decrepitude of old age or by human disease, death soon follows.

Plumb

Plumbum was the Latin for lead, and was used also of a scourge with a blob of lead tied to it, of a line with a lead ball at its end for testing perpendicularity, etc., the source of our plumb, plumber, plunge, plump, plumbago, plummet, etc. A plumb-line is accordingly a line, or cord, with a piece of lead at the bottom to pull it taut, used to test vertical walls with the line of gravity, hence, by a simple expansion of reference, an emblem of uprightness.

Up means up, right means straight; an upright man

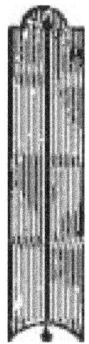

is one who stands straight up and down, doesn't bend or wabble, has no crooks in him, like a good solid wall that won't cave in under pressure.

Poor

Almost from the moment that a candidate for Freemasonry crosses the threshold of the Lodge, the duty of rendering aid and sustenance to those who lack in this world's necessities is urged upon him.

Porch

The Great Porch of the Temple of Solomon was magnificent and expansive, and its value to the appointments and uses of the Temple was invaluable. Hence, this porch is given a distinctive recognition in the ritual and teachings of Masonry.

Pot of Incense, The

is an emblem of a pure heart, which is always an acceptable sacrifice to the Deity; and, as this glows with fervent heat, so should our hearts continually glow with gratitude to the great and beneficent Author of our existence, for the manifold blessings and comforts we enjoy.

Prayer

Petitions to Deity in behalf on one's own needs, intercessions for others, communion with God, and prayer in all its elements of praise and worship are fundamentals in the tenets of Freemasonry. From the time a candidate crosses the threshold of the Lodge to the topmost Degree in Masonry, the privilege and duty of prayer are urged upon him, and every step is taken in a Holy atmosphere of Divine worship.

Preparation

In all the work of Freemasonry, emphasis is placed upon the importance of adequate preparation of moral, ethical and spiritual vocations. Preparation of the heart is the first essential in Masonry, and certain outward preparations symbolic of, and manifesting, inward preparedness are required.

Profane

This has a technical meaning in Masonry, nevertheless it adheres closely to the original significance of the word. *Fanum* was the Latin for temple; pro meant "before," in the sense of "outside of." It is the picture of man standing on the outside, not permitted to enter. It has this same sense in Masonry; the "profane" are those men and women who stand outside of Masonry. The word here, of course, has nothing to do with profanity in the sense of sacrilegious language.

Prudence

Growing out of the cardinal virtues which are emphasized throughout the degrees of Masonry is the practice of prudence by which we are instructed to regulate our conduct by the dictates of reason and in obedience to the cardinal virtues of faith, hope and love.

Q

Qualification

Qualify comes from the same word as quality. The root of it is the Latin *qua*, preserved in our "what." The quality of a thing was its *whatness*, the stuff of which it was made, its nature. The *fy* in "qualify" is from *facere*, to make, so that "qualify" means that a thing is made of the required stuff; and qualification means the act by which a thing is made of the required nature, or is declared to have it. The candidate for the Degrees of Masonry must possess certain characteristics in his nature; must be a man of lawful age, etc., and these are his qualifications.

Quarry

The Latin *quadratum* was a square; originally, quadrate and quarry meant the same. The word became applied to the pit from which rock is hewn because the principal task of workmen therein was to cut, or square, the stones; hence, literally a quarry is a place where stone-squaring is done. In Masonry "quarry" sometimes refers to the rock pits from which Solomon's workmen hewed out the stones for his Temple; at other times it refers to the various arenas of Masonic activities, as when it is said of an active Lodge member that "he is a faithful laborer in the quarry."

Quorum

Parliamentary law provides that a deliberative Body shall not proceed to business until a quorum of its members is present. This law is generally applicable to Freemasonry. According to common ritualistic rules, seven constitute a quorum, for work or business, in an Entered Apprentice's Lodge, five in a Fellow Craft's, and three in a Master Mason's. In addition, many lodges require that that either the Master or one Warden be present before a lodge can open.

R

Raised

In the Anglo Saxon *arisan* was used for any motion up or down, but in English it became used only of an upward motion, as in arise, rising, raise, rear, etc. Raise means to hoist, or carry, or lift, a body upward in space. There is no need to explain to a Mason why it is said of a candidate who has completed the Third Degree that he has been "raised," or why the climactic ceremony in that Degree is described as "raising." One is "initiated" an Entered Apprentice, "passed" a Fellowcraft, "raised" a Master Mason.

Refreshment

Friscus, or *frescus*, in the Latin had the meaning of new, fresh, recent; the *re* meant again; so that refresh means to renew, to make over, to undo the ravages of use and time, in Shakespeare's phrase, "to knit up the raveled sleeve of care." To "pass from labor to refreshment" is to find rest and recreation so as to undo the wearing effects of toil, as when a laborer knocks off at noon to eat his lunch and have a rest.

Regular

The Latin *rex*, king, sovereign, ruler, was a root from which many words have sprung, regal, royal, etc.; the Latins themselves had *regula*, or rule, and *regere*, to rule or govern. From this source has come our "regular." It means a rule established on legitimate authority. In Masonry "regular" is applied to those rules which have been established by Grand Lodges and Grand Masters. A "regular Lodge" is one that conforms to Grand Lodge requirements; a "regular Mason" is the member of such a Lodge who conforms to its laws and bylaws.

Relief

To relieve the distressed is a duty incumbent on all men, but particularly on Masons, who are linked together by an indissoluble chain of sincere affection. To soothe the unhappy, to sympathize with their misfortunes, to compassionate their miseries, and to restore peace to their troubled minds, is the great aim we have in view. On this basis we form our friendships and establish our connections.

Reverence for God

The very nature of God, His attributes and qualities, His creation, preservation and sovereignty over man, His redemptive grace and love, even His name, demands of man a reverent attitude at all times. God, Himself, and His name which stands for his personality, supremacy, majesty and glory are always revered in the Lodge of Masons, and the same attitude toward God should characterize the personal life of every true Mason. Anything and everything that represents God to the mind of man should be held sacred.

Right

This, one of the noblest words in the English language, is also one of the oldest, being found in the very ancient Sanskrit in the form *raj* meaning rule. It appeared in Latin as *rectus*, meaning direct, straight, a rule,— rule being used in the sense of our ruler, a device for drawing a line which is the shortest distance between two points. Such words as regent, rail, direct, rector, rectify, rule, came from this Latin term. Right means "straight," as in a "right line," a "right angle," etc.; through a familiar metaphorical application it has come to stand for conduct in conformity with moral law. Our "rights" are those privileges which strict law allows to us. A "horizontal" is a right line on the level; a "perpendicular" is a right line up and down, or at right angles to the horizontal. "Right" and "regular," discussed just above, originally were close together in meaning.

Rite

a system of Masonry beginning in the craft lodge and concluding in a final degree. A arrangement of Masonic degrees. "Rite," like "right," is very old; it has been traced to the if Sanskrit *riti*, meaning usage, which in turn was derived from *ri*, meaning flow, suggesting the regular current of river. In Latin this became *ritus* meaning in general a custom, more particularly a religious custom, or usage. Masonry has had many rites, some existing for only a short period of time.

Ritual

In Masonry the ritual is the prescribed set of ceremonies used for the purpose of initiation. It should be noted that a set of ceremonies does not become a ritual until it has been prescribed by some official authority, as a Grand Lodge.

Royal Art, The

the art of building in former times (architecture); it is used today as to designate Freemasonry as well.

S

Sabbath Day

Freemasonry recognizes man's constitutional requirement for one day's rest from the ordinary secular toils of life, and accepts as part of its fundamental teachings of the Divine establishment of the Sabbath Day. By legendary instructions, through symbolisms, and by precept, the privilege and duty of Sabbath observations are inculcated. The Sabbath Day is honored as an allotted period for rest and Divine Worship.

Saints John

Saint John the Baptist and Saint John the Evangelist are the two patron saints of Freemasonry in the USA.

Sanctuary

Holy places dedicated to the services and worship of God are a necessity for man. They are to be revered even as the name of God and utilized by man for his spiritual culture and for communion with the Most High. Moses erected a Sanctuary under the directions of God, and Holy places for worship have been perpetuated ever since. In the Bible, this name is ascribed to the Most Holy Place in the Tabernacle and in the Temple.

Sanctum Sanctorum

the Latin phrase referring to the Holy of Holies or innermost chamber of King Solomon's Temple where the Ark of the Covenant was kept.

Scottish Rite

a 33 degree system created in 1801 in Charleston, South Carolina and came to be known as the Ancient and Accepted Scottish Rite. While the system has 33 degrees, it is normally worked in the U.S. from the 4th to 33rd degree. Only a very few craft lodges in the U.S. work in this ritual (mostly in Louisiana). Outside the U.S. it is a very popular ritual used in craft lodges and well as the bodies working the higher degrees of the rite.

Scripture Readings

It is not only required that the VSL on the altar in the Lodge be spread open as a necessary preparation for opening the Lodge and during its work, but that it be opened at certain passages during the several Degrees. For the First Degree, the assigned passage is normally Psalms 133; for the Second, Amos, chapter 7; in some jurisdictions, 1 Corinthians, chapter 13, and for the Third, Ecclesiastes, chapter 12.

Seal

This, like our words "sign" and "insignia," is derived from the Latin *sigillum*, diminutive of *signum*, meaning a mark, or sign. It is some kind of device affixed to a document in place of a signature or in close connection with a signature for the purpose of showing that the document is regular or official. A document bearing the seal of a Lodge shows that it is officially issued by the Lodge, and not by some irresponsible person or persons. The word is also used for the tool by means the device is stamped into wax, or whatever similar material may be used for the purpose.

Secrecy

From *Se*, apart, and *cernere*, separate, the Latins had *secretum*, suggesting something separated from other things, apart from common knowledge, hidden, covered, isolated, hence "secrecy." There is a fundamental difference between "secret" and "hidden," far whereas the latter may mean that nobody knows where a thing is, nothing can be secret without at least one person knowing it. The secrets of Freemasonry are known to all Masons, therefore are not hidden; they are secrets only in the sense that they are not known to profanes. A similar word is "occult," which means a thing naturally secret, one, as it were, that secretes itself, so that few can know about it. See also the paragraphs on "clandestine" and "mystery" in the preceding pages. There is also another less familiar word in Masonry meaning hidden, covered up, concealed, secret; it is pronounced "hail" but is spelled "hele."

Secretary

The present use of this word has departed widely from its original meaning. The Latin *secretus* meant secret, private; *secretarium* was a conclave, a caucus, a council behind closed doors, consequently a *secretarius* was some very confidential officer, and was used of a secretary in our sense, of a notary, a scribe, etc. Since the handling of correspondence and the keeping of records is usually a confidential service the man who does it has come to be called a secretary. The secretary of a Lodge cares for all its correspondence and its records.

Self Support

the duty of supporting one's self and his family by individual initiative and personal labor is a universal tenet of Freemasonry.

Senior Warden

The "Second in Command" of a lodge. Similar to "First Vice-President" in other organizations.

Shibboleth

A word used by followers of Jephthah to test certain of the Ephraimites who sought to escape across the Jordan after having refused to fight in the armies of Israel was *Shibboleth*. Because of their Ephraimite dialect, they pronounced it *Sibboleth*.

Shod

wearing footgear, with shoes on, not barefoot

Sideliner

a Mason who, when attending a Masonic meeting, is not sitting as an Officer of the Lodge.

Sign

This comes from the Latin *signum*, a word which appears in a dozen or more English words, as signature, signet, signify, consign, countersign, resign, etc. Where a seal is used principally on documents and for the purpose of showing them to be official, sign is used much more variously and widely; it is some kind of gesture, device, mark, or design which indicates something, or points to something, and which often has a meaning known only to the initiated. Masonic signs are gestures that convey a meaning which only Masons understand, and which most frequently are used for purposes of recognition.

Silver Cord

"Or ever the silver cord be loosed" is a figurative expression in the beautiful passage descriptive of the delibitations of old age or approaching death. It is thought to refer to the weakening of the spinal cord which results in the loosening of the nervous system.

Solomon

Solomon was the son of David and Bathsheba, and David's successor on the throne of Israel. Though not the oldest of David's sons, he was chosen by his father to be his successor and was crowned king prior to David's death, when only about twenty-one years of age. He was solemnly charged by his father to build the Temple for which large funds had already been gathered. Solomon prayed especially for wisdom which was given to him by God above the measure of any other man in history. The league made with Hiram, King of Tyre, by his father was perpetuated, and by his assistance the Temple was carried to completion within seven and one-half years, beginning the fourth year of his reign.

Speculative

The Latin *specere* meant to see, to look about; *specula* was a watchtower, so called because from it one could look about over a wide territory. It came to be used metaphorically of the mental habit of noting all the aspects of a subject; also, as applied to theoretical knowledge as opposed to practical skill. "Speculative Masonry" was knowledge of the science, or theory, of building; "Operative Masonry," trained skill in putting that knowledge into practice. When Operative Masonry was dropped out of the Craft in the eighteenth century, only the speculative elements remained and these became the basis of our present Fraternity. It is for this reason that we continue to describe it as Speculative Masonry. The word has nothing to do with philosophical speculation, or with theorizing merely for its own sake.

Spiritual Temple

Freemasonry draws many sublime lessons and deduces many worthy truths from the symbolisms of the building of King Solomon's Temple, as well as from operative Masonry and architecture respecting the more important superstructure of moral, ethical and spiritual components knows as the Spiritual Temple. The building of this Temple is in vain without Divine aid. It fact, it must be built with God as the Chief Architect, and all the material that goes into it must pass His inspection and approval.

Square

The Latin *quad ratum* was a square. *Quatuor* meant "four;" from it we have square, four, quad, quadrangle, squadron, etc. In geometry a square is a four-sided straight-lined figure having all its sides equal and all its angles right angles; and since early carpenters and Masons had to use an instrument for proving the angles to be right, they fell into the habit of calling that instrument a square. In Masonry the square is used in at least three distinct senses; as a sharp instrument, as a working tool, and as a symbol, the last named when used with the compasses on the Holy Bible. As a symbol it refers to the earth, for so long a time supposed to be square in shape; as a working tool, it refers to all those forces by means of which one prepares himself to fit into his own proper place in the Brotherhood, like a Perfect Ashlar in a wall.

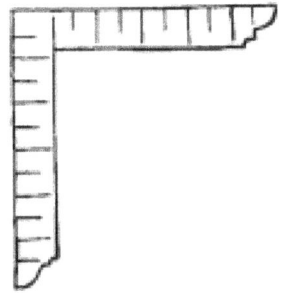

Stand To and Abide By

This is a unique pledge of every mason and means that he binds himself to stand by and obey every regulation of the Order, that he will be governed at all times by its laws and rules, and that the landmarks of the Fraternity will be followed faithfully in every detail.

Steward

This came into general use through the church, in which it was adopted as the name for an important official and also for an important theological doctrine; the doctrine of stewardship. The word itself had a peculiar origin. In Anglo Saxon *stigo* was a sty or place in which domestic animals were kept; a *weard* (see "warden") was a guard, or keeper; therefore the steward was the keeper of the cattle pens. Its meaning became enlarged to include the duties of general over-seer, one who is in charge of a household or estate for another; and still more generally, one who provides for the needs for food, money, and supplies. In the history of Masonry the office of steward has performed a variety of functions; the caring of funds, distribution of charity, preparing for banquets and similar services.

Subdue

to quiet or bring under control by physical force or persuasion; to reduce the intensity or degree of; tone down.

Sublime

Sublimis, in Latin, referred to something high, lofty, exalted, like a city set on top of a hill, or an eagle's nest atop some lonely crag. It refers to that which is eminent, of superlative degree, moral grandeur, spiritual exaltation. Inasmuch as the Third Degree is at the top of the system of Ancient Craft Masonry, it is known as "The Sublime Degree.

Superfluity

overabundance; excess; immoderate, especially living habits or desires.

Summons

Like the word *monitor*, explained some pages back, summons is derived from the Latin term of which the verb was *monere*, meaning to warn, or to remind, as in "admonish"; the "sum" is the combining form of *sub*, under, or privy to, in the secret of, as in the old phrase "sub rosa." A summons is an official call sent out by persons in authority to some person acknowledging that authority to appear at some place, or to perform some duty; in other words a person who is "on the inside," who is a member, is admonished by his superiors, and must obey under penalty. The duty involved and the penalty attached distinguishes a summons from a mere invitation. A Lodge, Grand Lodge, or some official issues a summons; a Mason is under obligation to respond to either, if it be due, official, or regular.

Superstructure

anything based on, or rising from, some foundation or basis; an entity, concept or complex based on a more fundamental one.

Sword Pointing to a Naked Heart

The "Sword Pointing to a Naked Heart" demonstrates that justice will sooner or later overtake us; and although our thoughts, words, and actions may be hidden from the eyes of man, yet that the All-Seeing Eye, whom the sun, moon, and stars obey, and under Whose watchful care, even comets perform their stupendous revolutions, pervades the inmost recesses of the human heart, and will reward us according to our merits.

Symbol

It is interesting to compare this word with "emblem" with which it is so often confused. The Greek *symbolon* was a mark, or sign, or token, or tally; it is derived from sun, together, and *ballein*, put, or throw, from which we have ball, ballistics, etc. *Symbolon* indicated two things put together, thrown together, or matched together. If, for example, the numeral 9 is matched to a pile of marbles, one to one, the 9 is a symbol of the number of marbles. From this came the custom of calling a symbol some object, device, design, picture, etc., used not for its own sake, but for the purpose of referring to some other, and perhaps very different, thing with which it has been associated. It is any visible, audible, or tangible object used to typify some idea, or truth, or quality, as when a wedding ring is made the symbol of marriage, the square is made the symbol of the earth, or the cross is made the symbol of Christianity, the crescent of Mohammedanism, etc.

T

Tabernacle

This was a moveable structure built under the directions of Moses at Mount Sinai according to the pattern given to him by God in a special revelation. In its truest sense, the Tabernacle was a representation of the presence of God in the midst of Israel, and the central place for worship. This is the model Solomon used to build his Temple.

Table of Shewbread

This article of furniture in the Tabernacle was a table made of acacia wood and of the ordinary make-up with legs. It was furnished with dishes, bowls, spoons and covers, all made of pure gold. Upon this table was placed twelve cakes of bread made of fine flour, in two rows of six cakes, called shewbread (also referred to shewbread). These cakes or loaves were removed every Sabbath and fresh bread supplied in their place. Only the priests were allowed to eat this removed bread. In King Solomon's Temple, instead of just one table, ten were used. They were patterned after the table of the Tabernacle, except they were made of pure gold and were much larger.

Temple

King Solomon's Temple holds a place of universal and pre-eminent interest due, in great measure, to Freemasonry which has kept alive through the centuries many fascinating legends and romances, innumerable symbols and rituals, a goodly number of rites and ceremonies associated with the building of the Temple and with its history. It is interesting to note that in Masonic nomenclature the ideal life, here and hereafter, is described metaphorically as a temple, one of a thousand examples of the extent to which Freemasonry is saturated with religious language and emotions.

Temple Builder

The legend of the Temple builder which forms a significant feature of the Third Degree in Freemasonry and the basis of profound lectures has been an essential part of Masonic ritual and Degree work throughout the history of the Order. Its authenticity cannot be questioned nor can its importance in the rites of Freemasonry be overestimated.

Temple of the Body

The symbolism of Solomon's Temple in the science of speculative Masonry, and the several rites of the Order based upon operative Masonry in the construction of the Temple, are intended to convey and inculcate great moral, ethical and spiritual truths. Among these truths is the teaching that man's body is to be made a fit Temple for the indwelling of God, and than many of the symbolisms in the building of King Solomon's Temple find their realities in human life and experience.

Temperance

moderation in action, thought or feeling; self-restraint; a habitual moderation in the indulgence of the appetites or passions; moderation in, or abstinence from, the use of intoxicating substances.

Ten Commandments

Masons recognize and honor the Decalogue incorporated in the laws of Moses as being of Divine origin and accept them as the moral code by which all human relations with God and with mankind should be regulated.

Testimony

Evidence in support of a fact or assertion; proof. In ancient Israel and other societies, the putting off of the shoes was a testimony of reverence for God or for an earthly superior, and as a token of confirmation in making contracts with fellowmen. The practice in certain rituals of Masonry may be traced back to this ancient custom.

Three Chambers

The upper, middle and lower chambers of King Solomon's Temple were rooms adjoining the main building fitted for quiet communication with God, as places for the preparation of priests and for storage of Temple vessels and instruments.

Three Principal Supports

As Masons we are taught that a Lodge has three principal

supports or pillars, denominated Wisdom, Strength and Beauty. The pillar of Wisdom (to contrive) on the right, the pillar of Strength (to support) on the left, and the pillar of Beauty (to adorn) in the center.

Three Steps, The

usually delineated upon the Master's carpet, are emblematical of the three principal stages of human life, viz.: Youth, Manhood, and Age. In Youth, as Entered Apprentices, we ought industriously to occupy our minds in the attainments of useful knowledge; in Manhood, as Fellow Crafts, we should apply our knowledge to the discharge of our respective duties to God, our neighbor, and ourselves; that so, in Age, as Master Masons, we may enjoy the happy reflection consequent on a well-spent life, and die in the hope of a glorious immortality.

Tiler (Tyler)

In operative Masonry, the workman known as the Tiler placed over the finished edifice a roof of tiles, and thus provided protection for the building. The symbolism of his work is invested in the office of Tiler (spelled Tyler in some jurisdictions) in speculative Masonry. His duty is to provide protection for the Lodge when it is organized and ready for business, closing the doors, keeping away eavesdroppers and intruders, and guarding the sacred precincts from intrusions of any kind.

Token

This is from the Greek *deigma*, meaning example, or proof—the origin of the word "teach," and in its orginal sense had much the same meaning as sign and symbol, for it was an object used as the sign of something else. It is generally used, however, in the sense of a pledge or of an object that proves something. In our usage a token is something that exhibits, or shows, or proves that we are Masons—the grip of recognition, for example.

Tongue of Good Report

having a good reputation; those who know you report that you are a good man; a credit to yourself and to society.

Troubles of Life

Freemasonry recognizes the fact that man in his sin-fallen state is the natural heir to sufferings, frailties, weaknesses, trial and troubles; and that release and renewal of strength may be found only in God and the use of the means of Divine Grace and Providence.

Trowel, The

is an instrument made use of by operative Masons to spread the cement which unites the building into one common mass; but we, as Free and Accepted Masons, are taught to make use of it for the more noble and glorious purpose of spreading the cement of brotherly love and affection; that cement which unites us into one sacred band or society of friends and brothers, among whom no contention should ever exist, but that noble contention, or rather emulation, of who best can work and best agree.

Trust in God

In this life, mans knows not what an hour or a day may bring forth. Paths upon which he must travel are unknown, and many unseen and unexpected dangers await him. Even when among friends, there is a constant need for Divine wisdom, sustenance, strength, aid and guidance. Hence, as the candidate crosses the threshold of the Lodge, and throughout all the ceremonies and rites of Freemasonry, he is required to "put his trust in God."

Truth

Truth is a divine attribute and the foundation of every virtue. To be good and true is the first lesson we are taught in Masonry. On this theme we contemplate, and by its dictates endeavor to regulate our conduct. Hence, while influenced by this principle, hypocrisy and deceit are unknown among us; sincerity and plain dealing distinguish us; and with heart and tongue we join in promoting each other's welfare and rejoicing in each other's prosperity.

Tubal-cain

The son of Lamech, a descendant of Adam through the Cainite line, Tubal-cain is regarded in Masonry as the father of skilled workmanship in artistic productions for building purposes.

Tuscan

one of the five orders of architecture, originated in the Tuscany area of southern Italy.

Twenty-Four Inch Gauge

is an instrument made use of by operative Masons to measure and lay out their work. But we, as Free and Accepted Masons, are taught to make use of it for the more noble and glorious purpose of dividing our time. It, being divided into twenty-four equal parts, is emblematic of the twenty-four hours of the day, which we are taught to divide into three parts, whereby we find a part for the service of God and a distressed worthy brother; a part for our usual vocations; and a part for refreshment and repose.

U

Unity

The mystic tie of true fraternalism is love. But, even where brotherly love prevails, differences of opinion, conflicting ideas, unenlightenment on the part of some, prejudices and varied interests in life endanger the spirit of genuine fellowship and unity. Hence, Masons are constantly taught to avoid "confusion among the workmen," discord, strife, jealousies and vain discussions on non-essentials; and to cultivate zealously and fervently the spirit of true unity in the Lodge and in the Fraternity.

Undiscovered Country From Whose Bourne No Traveler Returns

that which lies beyond death; the afterlife (Shakespeare, *Hamlet*: Act III, Scene 1)

Usual Vocation

your job or profession; the manner in which you make your living.

Untempered Mortar

The use of mortar not composed of the correct ingredients or in which these ingredients are improperly mixed in operative Masonry is certain to result in a weak and defective building, in a building that will soon disintegrate and tumble down. In speculative Masonry, such untempered mortar is symbolic of dishonest and fraudulent mixtures in the building of character or in the construction of the institution of Freemasonry. It represents hypocrisy, the representation of evil as good, the employment of bad materials in moral, ethical and spiritual architecture.

V

Veiled Allegory

Uttering a thing in parabolic form (i.e., parable) with its meaning hidden. Many of the sublimest truths of Freemasonry are thus spoken, and even those who have been given the mysteries of speculative science must delve into the caverns of Masonic mystery to gather these hidden gems of truth.

Veil of the Temple

This was the curtain or partition which separated the Holy Place from the Most Holy Place. It served as a constant reminder to worshippers than only the High Priest, and he only once a year after having made proper atonement for his own sins and for the sins of the people, was allowed to enter the Holy of Holies. As a result of the atonement of Christ in his death on the cross, this veil was rent and destroyed, and through Him as High Priest an open door into the Heavenly Sanctuary has been prepared for all true worshippers.

Vicissitudes

the successive, alternating or changing phases or conditions of life or fortune; ups and downs; the difficulties of life; difficulties or hardships which are part of a way of life or career

Vide Aude Tace

Latin for: *See, Dare, Be Silent*

Vide Audi Tace

Latin for: *See, Hear, Be Silent*

Virtus Junkxit Mors Non Separabit

Latin for: *Whom Virtue Unites, Death will not separate*

Visitors

The laws of ancient Israel with respect to the treatment of strangers or visitors have full recognition and force among Freemasons. In fact, no Mason is allowed to regard as a stranger or visitor any Brother Mason, even though he has no acquaintance with him, and even if he may be of some other religion, country or nationality.

Vouch

to give personal assurances; give a guarantee. This harks back to the Latin *vocare*, to call, to summon, and is the origin of voice, vouchsafe, vocation (in the sense of a "calling"), vocal, etc. To vouch is to raise one's voice in testimony, to bear witness, to affirm, to call to witness. If we vouch for a brother we raise the voice to testify that we know him to be a regular Mason.

Vouchsafe

to condescend to grant or bestow (a privilege, for example); deign.

Vows

The "vows of a Mason" are the inward and spiritual covenants of the mystic ties of the Fraternity which have their outward expression in the formal obligations assumed in the several Degrees of the Order. The vows are the covenants of heart and conscience which serve as the main force of heart and character in faithfully observing the obligations verbally expressed before the altar.

W

Wages

Wage, of which wages is the collective plural, remotely descended from the Latin *vas*, having the meaning of pledge, security, pawn, or a promise to pay backed up by security. After it entered into modern languages it had a peculiar history; it became *gage*, a pledge or pawn, appearing in our engage, disengage, etc., but having no relation with gage, one of our Working Tools; "wager" in the sense of a bet; in another context it became "wed," the act of marrying, so called because of the pledges given; and "wage" in the sense of compensation for service given. An "allowance" is a one-sided form of payment, depending on the will of the giver; a "stipend" is a fixed sum, usually nominal, and is supposed to be paid as per a permanent arrangement; a "salary" (from *sal*, or salt, the old pay given soldiers) is an amount fixed by contract, and estimated over a relatively long period of time, year or month; "wages" are paid to laborers over short periods of time, or at the completion of the required task. It is certain that the operative Masons who labored in the construction of King Solomon's Temple were paid wages, but there is no Biblical reference as to the daily wage paid. In Speculative Masonry the Master Mason symbolically receives "wages," rather than salary, because they represent the rewards that come to him as rapidly as he does his work; and, as the etymology of the word suggests, they are certain, something one may bank on.

Warden

"Ward" is of Medieval origin, having been used in early English, French, German, etc., always in the sense of to guard something, a meaning preserved in warden, guard, guardian, wary, ware, ward, etc. A warden is guardian of the west gate of the Temple, the Junior Warden of the south gate.

Warrant

This also derives from the same source, and carries the general meaning of "to defend," "to guard." Warrant is sometimes used as a pledge of security; in Masonry it is a document officially issued to authorize the formation of a Lodge, and consequently acts as the pledge, or security, for the future activity of it.

Wayfaring Man

A traveler or transient, one with no settled home, is often referred to as a wayfaring man.

White

White is symbolic of purity in its various uses in Masonry.

White Stone

The white stone is a token of fraternal friendship and helpfulness as well as enduring alliance.

Widow's Son

Masons are sometimes referred to as "sons of the widow" as this was the title applied to Hiram, chief architect of Solomon's Temple.

Widows and Orphans

Masons are solemnly pledged to make special provision for widows and orphans in need, especially among families of the Fraternity.

Winding Stairs

The Temple of Solomon was equipped with an impressive winding stairway consisting of fifteen steps leading from the porch to the second floor. Elaborate and extensive symbolisms are attached to these winding stairs in the work of Freemasonry.

Wisdom of Solomon

In ancient Craft Masonry, King Solomon stands as the representative of the highest degree of wisdom. The East, the source of light, symbolizes for every true Mason the wisdom needed for success in life. The East is represented by the pillar that supports the Lodge and by the Worshipful Master.

Word

In all of its several and varied uses, the term WORD symbolizes Divine Truth. The search for the Word in any sense means ultimately the search for Truth. The whole system of speculative Masonry is, in its essence, the search for Truth. The written word of God hold a pre-eminent place in all Degrees of Masonry and in all of its teachings.

Worshipful

As used in Worshipful Master, from the Anglo-Saxon, worthship (worthy); honorable or respectable. Used as a respectful form of address. The term has no religious or sacred implication.

Y

Yod

A Hebrew letter equivalent in sound to I or Y. It is the initial letter of the word Jehovah, the Tetragrammaton, and hence was peculiarly sacred among the Talmudists. In Symbolic Freemasonry, the yod has been replaced by the letter G. But in the advanced Degrees it is retained, and within a triangle, as in the illustration, constitutes the symbol of the Deity.

York Rite

A system of Masonry termed by Albert Mackey (when worked in the U.S.) the *American Rite*. In the U.S., the York Rite begins in the craft lodge and continues to the degree of Knight Templar. Only a handful of lodges in the U.S. work any ritual other than the Webb based York Rite ritual.

Z

Zabulon

The Greek wording of Zebulun, the tenth son of Jacob. In the Royal Arch Zabulon represents one of the stones in the Pectoral or Breastplate.

Zaphnath-Paaneah

An Egyptian title given to the Patriarch Joseph by the Egyptian King under whom he was Viceroy. The name has been interpreted Revealer of secrets, and is a password in the old instructions of the Ancient and Accepted Scottish Rite.

Zeal

enthusiasm; diligence; eagerness and great interest in pursuit of something.

Zenith

That point in the heavens which is vertical to the spectator, and from which a perpendicular line passing through him and extended would reach the center of the earth. From of old the documents of the Ancient and Accepted Scottish Rite are dated "under the Celestial Canopy of the Zenith which answers to ---"; the latitude of the place whence the document is issued being then given to fill the blank space. The latitude alone is expressed because that indicates the position of the sun's meridian height. Longitude, however, is always omitted, because every place whence such a document is issued is called the Grand East, the specific spot where the sun rises. The theory implied is, that although the South of the Lodge may vary, its chief point must always be in the East, the point of the sun rising, where longitude begins.

Zion

Mount Zion was the southwestern of the three hills which constituted the high table-land on which Jerusalem was built. It was the royal residence and hence it is often called the City of David. The name is sometimes used as synonymous with Jerusalem.

www.ingramcontent.com/pod-product-compliance
Lightning Source LLC
Chambersburg PA
CBHW031508270326
41930CB00006B/309